A Cup of Comfort

for Teachers

Heartwarming stories of people who
mentor, motivate, and inspire

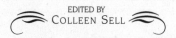

EDITED BY
COLLEEN SELL

ADAMS MEDIA
Avon, Massachusetts

D0816115

In memory of Mr. Robert Andes, and in gratitude to
Mr. William Brady, who believed in me when I did not.

Published by
Adams Media, an F+W Publications Company
57 Littlefield Street, Avon, MA 02322. U.S.A.
www.adamsmedia.com and *www.cupofcomfort.com*

ISBN: 1-59337-008-3

Printed in Canada.
J I H G F E D C B

Library of Congress Cataloging-in-Publication Data
A cup of comfort for teachers / edited by Colleen Sell.
p.   cm.
ISBN 1-59337-008-3
1. Conduct of life. I. Sell, Colleen.

This publication is designed to provide accurate and authoritative information
with regard to the subject matter covered. It is sold with the understanding that
the publisher is not engaged in rendering legal, accounting, or other professional
advice. If legal advice or other expert assistance is required, the services of a
competent professional person should be sought.

     —From a *Declaration of Principles* jointly adopted by a Committee of the
American Bar Association and a Committee of Publishers and Associations

Many of the designations used by manufacturers and sellers to distinguish their
products are claimed as trademarks. Where those designations appear in this
book and Adams Media was aware of a trademark claim, the designations have
been printed with initial capital letters.

Cover illustration by Eulala Conner.

This book is available at quantity discounts for bulk purchases.
For information, call 1-800-872-5627.

Acknowledgments

It is impossible to name everyone who made this book possible, for doing so would include not only each of the many people directly involved in the book's creation but also all of our teachers.

So, instead, I thank the authors who contributed their wonderful stories to this collection and the dedicated staff at Adams Media/F+W Publications, especially my right-hand comrades Kate Epstein, Beth Gissinger, Gary Krebs, Kate McBride, Laura MacLaughlin, and Gene Molter, for their outstanding contributions to A Cup of Comfort. And I will trust that each of these fine folks will find a way to thank their teachers personally.

I am most grateful to the many teachers who have given me both excellent instruction and inspiration. Though they are too numerous to name them all, I must at least acknowledge those whose mark on me has been nothing short of life-changing: Mrs. Justice, my second-grade teacher, who taught me to love learning. Mr. Burgess, my fifth-grade teacher, who nurtured both the curiosity of the scientist and the creativity of the artist within me. My high school teachers—Mr. Hurd, who helped me overcome my shyness enough to sing my heart out; Mrs. Fitz, who told me I'd be a writer someday and made me believe it; Mr. Andes and Mr. Brady, whose incredible support and guidance helped me to turn a very difficult corner without losing my balance. Bill Franklin, my dance instructor of more than a decade, who inspired me to dance and to live "my way." My college journalism professor, Lynn Milner, who taught me that true stories can be as creative and compelling as fiction. Chuck Smith, my anthropology and archaeology professor, whose brilliance and enthusiasm kept me coming back for more, simply for the joy of learning. And my beloved mentor and muse, the brilliant Richard Krevolin.

Heartfelt appreciation goes to my husband, Nikk, and to my family and friends, for their love and support, which sustains me in the long hours spent away from them and alone at my desk, reading and writing and editing.

Thank you, dear readers, for allowing us to share these comforting stories with you.

Contents

 Introduction

Teachers perform major miracles . . . daily.
—Meryl Streep

I never wanted to be a teacher. Not because I didn't like school or children; I loved school and I think kids are the best thing on the planet. I even like teenagers and young adults. And it's not because I've harbored any dislike or disrespect for education or teachers. I've always believed that teaching is one of the most honorable professions, and most of my teachers have been brilliant gems. But as the second in a line of six children—with four younger siblings to instruct in such important lessons as how to tie shoelaces, ride a bike, jump rope, act innocent, act cool, and not tick off adults—I realized early on that teachers get a lot of grief and not much glory. And as eager as I was to start school, by the third week of first grade—after my teacher realized I could already read and write (which I'd learned at the elbow of my older sister-teacher, Nita) and gave me the assignment of helping my classmates sound out "Go, Jill, go" and print their ABCs—I experienced firsthand just how frustrating and thankless a job teaching could be. While some students couldn't seem to "get" it, no matter how hard they and I tried, others were quite capable but didn't give a hoot. None of my tutees were enthusiastic about having a dorky teacher's pet as their tutor—and I paid for their displeasure on the playground. Right then and there, at age six, I realized I wasn't cut out for teaching . . . and decided to be a ballerina, instead.

Turns out I wasn't cut out to be a prima ballerina, either, as my dance instructor of many years, Bill Franklin, kindly pointed out to me when I was in my teens. I'd like to say I took his teacherly advice gracefully. But in my adolescent ignorance and indignity, I told him . . . well, let's just say I didn't tell him thank you. And I should have. Because he was a good teacher. And he was right: I wasn't good enough to dance professionally. He was also right several years later, when he asked me why I'd stopped dancing and I reminded him of his earlier dictum and he said, "Then you didn't want it badly enough. Otherwise, you wouldn't have let me or anyone else stop you." And with that, he gave me one last lesson that served me long after I'd lost the ability to dance *en pointe*.

Bill isn't the only teacher I have to thank. I am also grateful to my no-nonsense second-grade teacher, Mrs. Justice, for giving me work that challenged me, for relieving me of the anxiety-producing role of tutor to my peers, and for enabling me to enjoy learning. My joy in learning persisted throughout grammar school, junior high, high school, and college—thanks in no small part to numerous teachers whose skill, dedication, and ingenuity kept me challenged and interested.

As my three children made their way through school, I discovered another side of teaching: its rich rewards. I witnessed teachers who glowed with the satisfaction of seeing students blossom, both academically and personally, in the classroom and in their lives. I realized that the payback of teaching goes far beyond a paycheck: It comes from doing work that you enjoy, that challenges you, and that really matters, not only in the here and now with this year's students, but also in the long run, in what those students go on to do with their lives and in the world. Having school-age grandchildren has only increased my understanding of the allure and value of teaching. I stand in awe of and salute the millions who choose this honorable and gratifying profession, and who continue to empower their students with the power of education and to nurture the joy of learning.

A *Cup of Comfort for Teachers* celebrates inspirational teachers and the students and mentors who inspire them. I hope you enjoy their uplifting and insightful true stories. And I hope they inspire others to become teachers, too.

—Colleen Sell

Why I Teach

I know my students. Masses of awkward seventh graders swarm the halls of my rural middle school each day, hauling backpacks over one shoulder, talking and shuffling along the tile hallway floor from class to class. I watch them like a general from my post (my classroom door) and smile at the fact that I can call each one by name.

I know their secrets, their stories. Dora slouches and is shy, and I know it is because she spends all her time at home trying not to get noticed, so she won't feel the brunt of her stepfather's angry hand. Jay can pitch like a tenth grader, and all the girls swoon when he and his blond hair strut by, but I know he doesn't really even like baseball that much (he plays because his dad wants him to) and he is too scared to ask out the girl he likes. The kids think Keith is just the class clown, but I know of his dreams to become an astronaut (and I've recommended him for space camp). I know my students because I am their writing teacher. They trust me with their stories and so I am given the privilege of having a secret bond with each and every one of them.

I teach my students about the power of words, and I try to let them find release and expression through writing. We learn to trust each other in writing class because we learn how hard it is to write openly and honestly, and we learn that sharing your words takes courage. I see courage every day in my classroom, and I am always amazed at the words that come from my students' hearts.

One such example of courage took place during author's chair, a sharing session at the end of our writer's workshop in which students volunteer to share what they have written. We had a new student to the school, Al. Al was small and, with his dimpled cheeks and baby face, he looked younger than his classmates.

In fact, when Al was first introduced to the class two weeks earlier, one student said, "You're not in the seventh grade. You're a baby."

To that, Al quickly responded, "I'm Al Billslington, and I *am* in the seventh grade."

Despite his obvious courage, Al had been with us for only a short while and was still trying to fit in, so

I was a little surprised when he volunteered to read during author's chair. I had one of those teacher moments, when I smiled and nodded for him to read, while inside I said a silent prayer that the other students would not tease the new kid after he read. The room fell silent, and Al began to read.

"If I had one wish, it would be to meet my dad . . ." He started out loud and clear and held the attention of my usually restless seventh graders as he read on for what seemed like fifteen minutes. He told of how he had never known his father, who had left the family when Al was a baby. He shared the intimate details of his struggles to be the only man in the house at such a young age, of having to mow the lawn and fix broken pipes. He revealed to us the thoughts that raced through his mind constantly about where his father might be and why he might have left.

My eyes scanned the room for snickering faces of seventh-grade kids who I knew were prone to jump at a weakness and try to crack a joke, but there were no snickers. There were no rolling eyes or gestures insinuating boredom or pending attacks. All of my seventh-grade students were listening, really listening. Their eyes were on Al, and they were absorbing his words like sponges. My heart was full.

Al continued on, telling of nightmares at night, of never knowing a man so important to him, yet so unreal. I could hear his voice growing shaky as he read such passionate and honest words, and I saw a tear roll down one of his dimpled cheeks. I looked to the audience. There were tears on Jessica's face and on the faces of a few others seated quietly, intently listening.

They are letting him do this, I thought. *They are allowing him to share something he perhaps has never shared before, and they aren't judging him or teasing him.* I felt a lump in my own throat.

Al finished, struggling now to read his last sentence. "If I had one wish, it would be to meet my dad, so I wouldn't . . ." His tears were rolling now, and so were ours, ". . . so I wouldn't have to close my eyes in bed every night just wondering what he looks like."

Without any cue from me, the class stood up and applauded. Al smiled from ear to ear as they all rushed him with hugs. I was floored.

This is why I teach. I teach because I am allowed to learn the stories behind the faces. I teach because I can watch kids grow and laugh and learn and love. I teach because of students like Al.

—*Whitney L. Grady*

A Pair of Nothings

I held my breath as I watched my brother's finger trace through the newspaper listing of teachers assigned to third graders. I squeezed my eyes shut tight. *Please, please, don't let it be Miss Ball.*

"Miss Ball."

My brother's words hit me like a punch to the stomach. Wasn't it bad enough that third graders had to learn their multiplication tables before they could pass to fourth grade? No one wanted to be in Miss Ball's class to do it. She was scary.

According to my father, Miss Ball's badly scarred face was the result of smallpox in her youth. Knowing the cause didn't diminish the effect. Tall and slender, with eyes as black and shiny as onyx and lean fingers that could snap like a rifle shot, she was the most intimidating figure on the entire second floor.

That September I dragged my newly shod feet

into class, completely demoralized by my class assignment. With such a stern demeanor, Miss Ball would have even less of a sense of humor than the teachers I'd experienced previously. No tolerance for a creative imagination in her class. I prepared myself to hate every minute of the next nine months.

Reading was the first class. A breeze for me. My older brother Doug had taught me to read when I was four. Geography was a snap, too. Same with history. When we came back to the classroom after lunch recess, there it was on the blackboard: the first row of the dreaded multiplication table. The "zero times." The school chili gurgled in my stomach. By the end of the day, we would be repeating the numbers in that mindless prisoner-of-war style I had learned to resent from my first day of first grade. I planted my face on my fists.

Zero times zero made sense. I could even accept one times zero. But I had to question why two times zero was still zero. I was just a farm kid, but I knew when you had two of anything you had *something*. My hand shot up, wagging.

"Doesn't that two mean anything?"

Miss Ball stared at me, her black eyes unreadable. My classmates stared at me. I held my breath until my vision blurred. Maybe it really was possible to slither to the floor and sink into one of the cracks between those worn hardwood slats.

Then Miss Ball did something beyond my realm of experience. She smiled. A gentle smile. Not that evil smile teachers get when they sense a smart aleck in the class. I'd expected reproach. What I got was goose bumps. This was definitely new territory for me. Now everyone was staring at the woman at the front of the room and not at me. I could breathe again.

She turned to the blackboard and drew a large rectangle, which she divided into halves. "This," she said, pointing to the blank interior of the left block, "is a nothing. A zero." Next she gestured to include both portions of the divided rectangle. "And these are two nothings. Class, what do you get when you have one nothing and one nothing?"

"Nooothiiing, Miiiss Baaall."

I stared at that divided rectangle long after Miss Ball and my classmates had moved on to discuss other zeroes. A blank domino. A pair of nothings. I wanted to hug myself with delight. At last, a teacher who could illustrate a point, who could make me visualize rather than merely saying, "Just because." Even back then, before analysis of learning behavior became popular, she was perceptive about some students learning better through visual aids and reinforcement rather than auditory instruction.

In later lessons, when her personal stock of colored chalk appeared, I discovered Miss Ball could draw flowering trees with nests hiding in them, clouds with exotic birds flying around the sky, and rays of sunshine and rippling water with lily pads that looked real. She could write poems, too. Short poems with exciting new words that expanded my vocabulary and my horizons.

Miss Ball was a kindred soul. A creative soul. A beautiful soul.

Later in the year a box appeared on the activity table. It was full of 3-by-8-inch cards. On each card was a word. On the back of the card was the definition of that word. Nothing in my education to that point had ever struck such a spark of excitement. Words were some of my most favorite things in the world. I found words fascinating, not so much the sounds they made when you spoke them as their appearance, their meanings, how they could be employed in a sentence to alter meanings. These were all new words, big ones, 250 of them. This was not the vocabulary you learned on the farm. Not a single domestic animal resided in their midst. The box represented the lexicon of journalists, scholars, and philosophers.

Like a new kid in class, the words became my friends. I copied them, played with them, and introduced them into my conversation. And, like any other eight-year-old, I'm sure I mistreated them on occasion. I hardly noticed that none of my classmates shared my enthusiasm. The words were my companions on the baseball field and playground as well as in the library and the classroom.

Tears stung my eyes that final day with Miss Ball. I had more to learn from this wonderful teacher. She had so much more to teach. There were more boxes full of those musical, magical new words.

Fifty years have passed since I sat behind that old wooden desk with notches and initials carved by generations of students and darkened with decades of varnish, ink, and grime. Of all my teachers, I remember Miss Ball most, not for her flawed complexion and intimidating demeanor, but for her ability to spark the imagination of a dirt-poor, pig-tailed country girl. Thanks to Matilda Ball, the desire to learn burns as brightly for me today as it did when she drew that simple white-chalk rectangle filled with a pair of nothings.

—*Kathleen Ewing*

Guns and Roses

I retired from teaching after 3,100 students, 63,000 grades, 100 pairs of shoes, and 26 years in the classroom. I had seen everything—at least twice.

I began my career when women jammed their feet into pointy shoes, wrote with chalk, and hung decorations from the light fixtures—not easily accomplished balancing on three-inch steel rods the width of a fingernail. While I was talking about subject-verb agreement and prepositional phrases, permanent press replaced cotton and double knit replaced everything. There is an Illinois landfill still lumpy with my lime green Nehru jacket and skirt. While I was assigning lessons on Shakespeare, Tupperware modulated from clear lids to avocado to orange to mauve to turquoise to navy and slate blue. During my tenure, the first man walked on the moon, a president resigned, the *Challenger* exploded, and a robot explored Mars.

More important, it sometimes seemed, women began wearing pants. Administrators assaulted us with rules about our professional slackness, as if somehow a bell bottom on our leg diminished our ability to inspire thought and modify behavior. Heaven forbid that some rebel with a cause wore an outfit that didn't match top to bottom. Personally, I thought such wardrobe atrocities may have shot one's fashion sense in the foot, but they were hardly worth being sent home for something more color coordinated.

In the old days, I averaged grades by pencil on the backs of used envelopes. I advanced to a hand-crank adding machine to an electric one and to an expensive whiz-bang electronic calculator. By the end of my career, my grade book was a computer screen and back-up disk.

I taught fourth grade in a two-story brick elementary school. Cracks in the school's plaster walls formed patterns like the varicose veins my legs were acquiring. The ceiling rose twenty feet above the wood floor. The windows that stretched toward it were bigger than some movie screens. A silver radiator boiled and clanked with the seasons. It took longer to buckle into down jackets and galoshes than the twelve-minute recess I was supervising. I also taught in Missouri's largest school district the year all of its high school students shared one building. Half the student body attended between 6:30 A.M. and

12:30; the other half arrived for the 1:00 to 7:00 P.M. shift. The changeover, with 5,000 students swarming the horseshoe driveway, was not pretty.

We had bomb threats twenty years ago—usually in the spring. We'd evacuate the building, but we weren't really scared. We loitered on the sidewalk just outside the building that was supposed to blow up, talking, laughing, and joking. The only casualties in those afternoons in the sun were lessons on geometry or the Civil War.

I considered leaving teaching sometime after that. I didn't like the firing line where the general public, politicians, parents, and students came to doubt whether two college degrees and two decades in the classroom qualified me to teach. Their disdain pistol-whipped my enthusiasm. Shell shocked by the lack of respect, I (like many educators) was forced to barricade myself with lesson plans in duplicate, lists of phone calls made, and copies of progress reports sent. They filled two gray file cabinets in my room, simply because my word and my work weren't enough anymore.

Then education quantified itself into achievement scores. The alphabet spit out tests like a machine gun—the BEST, the MMAT, the CAT, the SRA, the ACT, and the SAT. I resented pinning my competency and reputation on four days of testing and on children who may simply be having a bad day because they overheard their parents fight or because they forgot to eat breakfast. Educators simply circled the wagons and shot themselves. I was one of the walking wounded.

Dress codes wearied me—again. Shoes without toes, it seemed, were professional; shoes without heels were not. Suspenders on a skirt were professional, but stylish overalls with a crotch were not. For twenty-four days of the month, jeans were not acceptable, but every payday, they suddenly were. Wardrobe no longer mattered to me. I wore my professionalism from the inside out. I got tired of dodging the bullets, the pellet-sized and hollow-pointed attitudes I couldn't see.

And then came Springfield, Littleton, and Jonesboro. The bullets became real, and reality checked into my school. A few days before the school year ended, a telephone call warned us: "The last day of school, somebody's going to die."

Faculty meetings weren't about tests or dress codes anymore. We discussed code words and procedures for hostage situations. We planned how to protect our students in the classroom and how to escape the building. We emptied student lockers and sent book bags home. The night before the last day of school, the building was searched and locked down tight.

The next morning, police patrolled the school grounds hourly. Their emblemed cars, starched uniforms, and holstered guns pierced a day that should have been buoyant with celebration. My twelve-year-olds entered the building through monitored entrances. They couldn't congregate in the gym for last-day conversations, but were sent straight to class. They quickly signed yearbooks and autographed T-shirts in the halls. The exits were locked. It was a grim day.

Then, halfway through the morning, Nick tapped me on the shoulder. I looked into a smile that spread from ear to ear. His pleasure lit the entire room. He laid a package, large enough for a weapon and long enough for a bomb, on my desk. Under the paper I carefully unfolded lay a single delicate white rose.

Nick had been one of my problem sixth graders. He had been a tight little rosebud himself, all wound up in his own world. He was determined to finish assignments first, impatient with classmates who were still working. He was the loudest and most self-righteous in class discussions. He lost his temper and dissolved in tears when confronted.

He and I had many conversations in the hall about his behavior. His mother and I conferenced over the phone and face-to-face, strategizing how to open his attention to other students' ideas and feelings. We were patient. We were firm. We were kind. Little by little, he blossomed. He read library books while others worked. He learned not to blurt out comments, not to contradict me, and not to interrupt others. His classmates elected him student council representative.

He applied, and was accepted, as a student office aide.

No test score recorded his progress, but on a day dirtied by apprehension, he was giving me a beautiful flower. I glimpsed his mother outside the door.

"Thanks for everything you've done for Nick," she told me. Then she hugged me. That was one parent contact I couldn't file. I murmured my pleasure at his gift. Nick and I finished out our day.

Nick's last day of school ended without incident. No bombs went off. No guns were fired. Students boarded yellow school buses and drove into their summer. I cleared my desk, picked up my rose, and left. When I got home, I found my most expensive crystal vase. Nick's flower deserved my best. It stayed on my dining room table opening wider and wider, as delicate and luminescent as the wafer moon.

Maybe we do live in a heavy metal world these days. Certainly education is still under fire, both from within and without. Its value continues to be equated with the assembly line, when learning should be much more than the parts of a sum. Still, when I think back over a career that's filled half my life, when the abrasions and contusions healed over, I remember my time in the classroom—not by the guns, but by the roses.

—*Vicki Cox*

Clown School

I lay in bed aching for a mental health day. I'd call the school secretary and croak out the words "strep throat." Thirty minutes later, she'd hiss into the intercom, "Listen up, speech students. No speech therapy today." The cruel news would not be welcome. At Thomas Jefferson Elementary School, speech was an exclusive club with very stringent membership requirements. My absence would especially upset James, the most zealous of my club members. James had coined the club slogan, "We Wove Peech!"

Picturing James' dejected face when the announcement of my demise was blatted over the intercom system, I reluctantly dragged myself out of bed. My morose sigh scattered flakes of cherry Pop-Tart across the mirror. Reasoning that rosy cheeks would clash with my blue funk, I skipped the makeup ritual and went straight to my closet. I pulled on gray slacks and an off-gray blouse—an ensemble that highlighted my Quaker gray, two-inch roots. Even my sterling silver earrings refused to shine. The mirror confirmed that my outward appearance was a precise reflection of my despondent soul.

Maybe a gaudy scarf would disguise my melancholy. In two minutes, a scarf with vast pink, purple, and teal psychedelic solar systems orbited my neck. I tied it into a flamboyant, 1980s-fashionable bow. Unfortunately, the ruse was useless. I still looked and felt abysmal. I jerked on my fleece parka, wool cap, and fur-lined mittens; spent ten minutes scraping the ice from my windshield; and cursed every irritating red light (six) between my house and Jefferson School.

James, red cheeked and runny nosed, greeted me at the door.

"Where you been, Miss Smiff? You wate."

Oh, why, oh, why had I come to school?

"I'm not late, James. You're early. Go back to your classroom."

"Nah. Miss Tim's wate too."

"James, Miss Kim is not late. I'm not late. You're early. Go eat breakfast."

"Nah."

He trailed me down the hall and into my classroom. The radiator pipes clanged. I dropped my overloaded satchel onto the floor; opened the closet door; and jerked off my coat, hat, and mittens.

"James, I need a cup of coffee. You'll have to go somewhere else."

"Nah. I just dough wif you."

"James"—I whirled around—"I'm not in the mood for early-morning visitors. You'll have to . . ."

"Wow! You wook pwetty, Miss Smiff."

"What?"

"You wook pwetty, Miss Smiff."

"Well," I stuttered, "Thank you, James."

"I wike a pwetty bow." His face lit up with a contagious smile.

I fluffed the harlequin bow and beamed a smile at him. "Really, James? I look pretty?"

"Weawwy pwetty, Miss Smiff."

"Well, thank you, James." Instantaneously, I felt better. Maybe I would get my mental health day, after all.

"You wook weal pwetty, Miss Smiff. You wook wike a cwown."

"What?"

"You wook wike a cwown, Miss Smiff! You weawwy do!"

I bit my tongue in an effort not to laugh. Tears rolled down my cheeks. When I could no longer hold it in, my laughter exploded with an unattractive snort.

James was puzzled. "What's wong, Miss Smiff?"

I knelt down beside him. "You make me so happy.

Guess what, James? I've been acting like a clown, too." (I should have said fool instead of clown.)

I still have my blue-funk days. Still occasionally feel the need to make a deathbed call to the school secretary. Still think of James, crawl out of bed, look in the mirror, and tell myself, "You wook wike a cwown, Miss Smiff."

For me, a mental health day is just a laughing matter.

—*K. Anne Smith*

Because It Matters

High school was pretty easy for me, and I wasn't alone. Everyone in the honors program typically cruised through our classes without breaking a sweat. The first month of honors American history class did nothing to challenge that expectation. Sure, we had a substitute from the first day on, but those first four weeks of memorizing names and dates were as easy, and as boring, as we'd all expected.

Mr. King came back just in time to give us the first test. He was a sight. He'd had a serious bout with hepatitis and was still frail and jaundiced from months spent recovering. His voice was just above a whisper, but he spoke with dignity and precision.

Even if he hadn't, we would have been riveted by his discussion of the results of that first test. After all, we were honors students. The question, though, wasn't whether we'd received an A; the question was who got the highest score.

The answer in this case was my friend Paul Larick. Paul was fiercely intelligent and fiercely competitive. He allowed himself to grin as Mr. King began with, "Mr. Larick, you earned the highest grade on the first test." His smile vanished when Mr. King went on to say, "You earned a D."

Mr. King paused to glance around the room, and to rest, before speaking again. "The rest of you," he said, "did not do so well, earning D-minuses or below."

"But—" someone said.

"That's not fair!" someone else cried.

"But you tested us on things we hadn't studied," a third person tried.

I don't remember who said these things. It wasn't me. I was too stunned to speak.

Mr. King looked at us. "The work you submitted," he whispered, "was not honors quality."

Mr. King was not unfair. He threw out all grades for the first test. He was not unkind. That was the last time he ever discussed grades publicly. And he was not without a sense of humor. He opened each class with an invitation of, "Does anyone have a good joke?" and closed class with "Questions? Comments? Obscure conundrums?" When someone shared a good joke, he often laughed so hard he fell over. When someone offered a good conundrum, he saluted its difficulty.

But what Mr. King was not, finally, was ever unclear about his standards, and that was a shock to us. We were all so used to getting As as a matter of course that we tried every strategy in the book to sway Mr. King.

"You graded my paper down for grammar and spelling. This isn't an English class," one of us would whine.

Mr. King would peer at us through or, if he was particularly testy, over his glasses and say, "Perhaps I should speak with Mr. Froelich about what you're learning in his English classes. If you apply your skills only in the classes in which they are studied, what good are they?"

I remember trying one such whine. "What do you mean, my thesis isn't supported? Isn't my idea original?"

Unblinking eyes gazed at me through a pair of heavy glasses. "Those two points are not, as I trust you know, related. Your idea is quite original. Daring, even. Now you need to support it."

Bitter, I tried again. "It would have been good enough in my honors English class."

"Well, it's not good enough here." Mr. King spoke quietly, to keep the matter private.

My answer was louder, an attempt to enlist the entire class behind me. "Well, why isn't it good enough?"

"Because my subject matter is important," he

said. "Because it is desperately important for you to learn your country's history—not just the names and dates, but the laws and debates behind the laws, their economic implications, and what the period perspectives were. Because it is desperately important for all of you to be able to form a cogent, well-supported argument that you deliver in clear, grammatically correct prose."

He had to rest then, but he went on when he could. "This is school, but if that's all it is, it's worthless. My standards are high because this matters."

After that, I would have followed him anywhere—and I would have killed to get an A in that class. But that, too, would have been the easy way out. Instead, I had to work. We had four textbooks for the class—economic, diplomatic, and military histories as well as a standard overall history of the United States. We also used primary sources.

We learned that just because an essay test was timed, that didn't mean one could cast aside a thesis statement or good organization. We learned history, but we also learned to research, to write, and to reason.

And because Mr. King did not play favorites and had reasons for all of his grading criteria, we learned two more things. We learned to stop thinking of grades as something personal and instead to use them to measure our performance of a given task.

And we learned the value of rigor in the service of an important goal.

These lessons were underscored by Mr. King's frail health. In every other class I'd had in which an instructor fell ill, the class had been made easier, allowing teacher and students to coast. Every time Mr. King stood up to explain something or held a position when challenged, the effort was visible and it underscored that primary explanation of his rigor: because it matters.

I didn't become a teacher until years later, but when a student asked a question late one semester, I realized how much Mr. King had influenced me.

"Hey, did you know we're doing more work in this class than they're doing in other freshmen English classes?" a student asked.

"Yes," I said. "By my estimate, you're doing thirty to forty percent more work in this class than the other sections are doing, and you're held to higher standards."

"You knew that?" he asked. "But why?"

Rather than answering directly, I waved a hand. "Pick someone. Anyone."

Mystified, he pointed hesitantly at one of his classmates.

"Do you like writing?" I asked.

"No," he said.

The first student winced.

I shook my head in agreement. "Never turn away from honesty. Now, the key questions: Do you like it more than you did? And are you better at it?"

"Yes," he said. "I used to hate it. Now, it's okay, and I tutor the guys in my frat on how to write papers."

I nodded. "Pick someone else."

He did, and we repeated the process. Some loved writing; some liked it; some still hated it but were teaching their friends to write. All had improved.

I returned the question to the student who had asked the question. "So, why are you held to higher standards in this class?"

"So we'll learn what we need to," he said.

"Exactly," I said. "Because it matters."

I went on to explain why they needed to be able to reason and to articulate their thoughts and opinions, but it wasn't my explanation. The words I spoke were James King's words, tumbling out halfway across the country and many years later. And they were still true.

—*Greg Beatty*

The Sound of One Door Opening

As a speech pathologist working in the public schools for twenty years, I have had the opportunity to work with many young children and their parents through our special education preschool programs. Some of these children are difficult to understand; some have very rudimentary language skills; some do not talk at all.

One child in particular stands out in my mind. Her name is Diana, and she was in a class of seven preschoolers. Diana had a broad face, wide-set eyes, a short stature, and an awkward gait. She had been born prematurely and had a plethora of health problems, including having had open-heart surgery and lingering heart problems. She had difficulties with motor skills, reasoning skills, and social skills. She also had a stubborn streak a mile long.

Diana was one of the students who did not talk.

She had developed her own means of communication, partly made-up sign language and partly pointing. She also had a system of grunts that she used to indicate she was hungry, that she wanted to go somewhere, and that she didn't want something. Like many parents, Diana's parents had been generally successful in interpreting her signs, grunts, and pointing, and they understood their child most of the time. However, there were still many times when they did not understand what Diana wanted. They also realized that Diana was far behind her peers in her language and many other skills.

Diana's mother brought her to and from school every Monday through Friday. Each time, Mom and I, or Mom and the teacher, would chat about what had happened in Diana's life the night before or what activities were coming up in Diana's life. We were always looking for something so exciting or so enticing that this little girl would want to attempt to communicate about it.

We tried sabotaging the environment by placing things within sight but out of reach, but Diana just looked at the item and then at the teacher. We had special treats and would "forget" to give her one. We would paint and give her a paintbrush but no paint; she was content to outwait us. We used mirrors and bubbles. We used new toys. We used computer-generated pictures. One parent brought in a live rabbit, and the children in the class were very excited. Several of the children squealed with delight or cried in fear of the big furry thing. Not Diana. She sat passively and looked while a teacher took her hand to stroke the rabbit.

Shortly after the rabbit incident, the teacher returned to school with photographs she had taken that day of the students and their precious reactions to the rabbit. When one of the photos dropped to the floor, Diana picked it up and stared at the child in the photo for an extraordinarily long time.

"That's Bobby," the teacher labeled.

As we watched, Diana handed the picture back to the teacher and continued to hold out her hand. Another photograph was placed in her hand, labeled by the teacher, and again she stared at it. This continued for each picture. Finally, the teacher took the photograph of Diana and whispered to us, "Let's see what she does with this." She handed it to the child and said, "This is Diana. This is you." Diana looked at the picture, then to the teacher. "Yes, Diana, that's you." She looked at the photograph again and finally smiled. We were elated. We had found something that Diana was interested in.

When we shared this with Diana's mom, she was equally excited. I think she went home and that same day took several rolls of film of toys, food, and other objects in their house, because two days later, Diana arrived at school with a mini photo album full of photographs. It was her new precious toy. During free time, she took it out of her backpack and looked at each picture and pointed and sometimes grunted. We offered her words in sign language, line drawings, and spoken words for each picture. Still, she didn't talk. But she was interested.

When she first brought her photo album to school, she was very possessive and if another child wandered in her direction while she was looking at the book, she quickly closed it and would lie down on it so no one could see it. Not until the other child left her immediate area would Diana sit up and open her book again. Eventually, Diana progressed from tolerating other students' peeks at her book to sitting side by side with a fellow student and having the book extended across both their laps. Sometimes, the other student would chatter away, often unintelligibly, and Diana would seem to listen to every sound, understanding it all.

Diana's favorite photographs were the ones of her family—her mom, dad, grandparents, her brother, Dave, and the family dog. Diana often patted those special photographs and smiled. How we wished we could get inside her head to know what she was thinking.

With two weeks of school remaining, things were winding down in that usual can't-wait-to-leave-but-there-is-too-much-to-do that all students and teachers feel. The structure in the classroom had become a little more relaxed, and playtime was a little longer than usual.

One morning Diana was lying on the floor with her book, poring over the family pictures. The other children were playing in different centers, and the room was fairly noisy with the prattle of a couple of the preschoolers. The teacher, working on the snack preparation, suddenly looked at me and asked, "What's that noise?"

I paused and gazed around the room, listening and wondering what could be producing the low hum that sounded like a small motor had been left on and was beginning to weaken. I circled the room, arrived at the spot where Diana was sprawled on the floor, and knelt down. My eyes widened as I realized that Diana was humming! I quickly lay down on the floor next to her and as unobtrusively as possible began to hum with her. As I tried to match her pitch, she slowly looked up at me and smiled. We continued to hum together at that one single pitch for a time. When I changed my pitch and tried to incorporate a tune, Diana quit humming.

Trying another tactic, I exaggerated the "mmm" and pointed to the picture of Diana's mom and then said, "Mmmmomm. Mom," repeatedly. Diana looked at me, at the picture, and then back at me. *Was I making sense to her?* I had no idea at the time whether I was or not. As much as we hated to stop, it was time for the children to go home.

We excitedly told Diana's mom what had happened, and she promised to pursue it. As the children all left, we teachers discussed that it was too bad the school year had to break for the summer for Diana, with this communication breakthrough seeming to loom on the horizon.

I remember vividly the next morning. I was late arriving to school and met Diana's mom in the hall as I walked into the building. She was crying. *Had something happened with Diana's heart?* I steeled myself for the worst and put down my bags.

"How is Diana? Is something wrong?" I uttered.

"No, no, nothing like that," Diana's mom said. She smiled and said, "I had to wait for you. To thank you."

"Why? What happened?" I was confused.

"This morning Diana woke up and climbed in my bed like she usually does. She stroked my cheek, smiled, and said, 'Mom.' She said 'Mom'! She said my name!"

We hugged and cried unabashedly in the hallway. We went into the classroom and cried some more with the teachers. As hard as we had worked to find an interest for Diana, it had been there all along. Working together as a team, we finally discovered the bridge across the void of silence in which Diana had been isolated. It was only one word and just the beginning, but it meant the world to Diana and her mom.

—*Paula Sword*

The First Day

Dozens of eyes stared at me. A sea of unfamiliar faces loomed large and forbidding. My teaching career was off to a nerve-wracking start. Terrified, I summoned the courage to smile. The appearance of several eager grins reassured me. Eyes and grins turned, expectant, and I knew I had to speak.

"Hello, boys and girls," I said, and introduced myself to the group of children standing in front of me. "I'm so glad you all came today."

My words sounded weak and small. *Project your voice,* I thought.

"This is such a special and exciting day—your first day of grade one."

Several children straightened their shoulders as if suddenly aware of their importance.

I directed my next comments to the intimidating row of parents lining the back of the room. Nothing in my education courses at university had prepared me for the folded arms, the candid looks of appraisal, and the eyes narrowed with suspicion. I was twenty years old, and I looked about fifteen. My shaky voice and nervous mannerisms had betrayed me. No wonder the parents were less than enthusiastic.

"Of course, the moms and dads are welcome to spend the morning with us," I said. "However, I'm sure some of you have other things you need to do."

Go home, I thought. *Please go home and leave me alone. I don't know about you, but I have the feeling I'm in the wrong place.*

No one moved. No one spoke.

"I'd be happy to answer any questions you might have," I said.

More silence.

I took a deep breath. "Perhaps we should get started."

I picked up a list of the students' names from my desk and began to read. "Tommy Adams. Are you here?"

A tentative hand went up, and I felt a flicker of relief.

"Tommy," I said. "Can you tell me your address and phone number?" In a moment of optimistic inspiration earlier that morning, I had decided not only to call the roll but also to check whether each child knew his home contact information.

Tommy frowned. "No," he said.

The flicker of relief I felt a moment earlier sputtered and died. I nodded.

"That's perfectly all right," I said, as Tommy's head drooped in defeat.

Great, I thought. *I ask the poor kid his first question, and he doesn't know the answer. Forget the phone numbers and addresses.* I glanced at the wrinkled paper clutched in my sweaty hand.

"David Allen, are you here?"

Another hand went up. His eyes glittered with excitement.

"I know my address and phone number," he announced with a triumphant glance at Tommy.

Tommy's eyes widened with indignation. "I know my phone number and address, too, David. I'm just not going to tell her," he said, pointing at me. "She's a stranger, and my mom told me never to tell a stranger my phone number or address."

Oh, God, I thought, *what ever made me believe I could be a teacher?*

There were mutters and whispers from the parents brigade at the back, and several mothers, after saying good-bye to their children, left the room.

Like rats leaving a sinking ship, I thought.

I gestured toward the rows of desks in front of me. "I'd like everyone to find their seat now. You'll find your name taped to the top right-hand corner.

I'll take the roll after you're all seated." *And just before I run screaming from the room.*

A few more mothers kissed their children goodbye, glanced my way as if to say, "My kid had better be in one piece when I get back," and departed.

The room came to life with excited chatter and the sounds of wooden chairs being pulled across the floor. Then, a child's mournful wail filled the room. In the corner, clinging to his mother's coat like a baby orangutan, was Tommy Adams.

"I want to go home," he sobbed. "I want to go home."

The room fell silent as everyone stopped to watch the drama. I reached out to touch Tommy's shoulder, and he flinched.

An apologetic look appeared on his mother's face. "He doesn't like new things, but he's never made a fuss like this."

I knelt down. In a soft, low voice, I attempted to comfort him. "It's all right, Tommy. Please don't cry. Everything's going to be okay."

I suppose I was consoling myself, too. This was not how I had pictured my first day of teaching, and a part of me wanted to howl and cry just like Tommy.

I tried bribing him. "Tommy, would you like to be in charge of picking out a story for me to read to the class?" I said.

His face buried in his mother's leg, he shook his head.

"Would you like to be my helper and collect the milk money?"

He hesitated for a moment this time, but after a few seconds, he shook his head again.

I glanced up at his mother. Her eyes and voice pleaded with me. "I have to get to work." This announcement provoked more crying from Tommy, this time louder and more desperate.

"Can I tell you a secret, Tommy?" I whispered.

I held my breath and waited. He stopped crying. He was listening.

"This is my first day, too," I said. "I'm new, and I'm kind of nervous and scared."

He turned around and stared at me, his red and swollen eyes full of incredulity. "You're scared?"

I shrugged and nodded. "A little. I've never been a teacher before, but you were in kindergarten, right?"

"Yes, I was. I used to get a sticker almost every day."

"I can tell just by looking at you that you're the kind of boy who would get a sticker almost every day." I reached out and held his hand. This time he didn't pull away. "I need your help," I said. "I could really use a friend. Someone who knows all about school. Someone like you."

A thoughtful look appeared on his face, and I gently squeezed the tiny hand. "Would you please stay and help me out?"

He sniffed, wiped at his eyes with one hand, and

nodded. With a silent prayer of gratitude, I stood up and led Tommy to his desk. When I glanced back at his mother, she smiled and nodded. I gave Tommy a gentle nudge. "Tell your mom you'll see her in a little while."

I held my breath as the little body stiffened, but then he turned around and waved. "Bye, Mom. See you after school."

I exhaled with relief and looked up at the clock. It was 9:30. Only two hours to go until lunch. I might just make it.

—*Susan B. Townsend*

Snapshots

Like most people, I collect photographs in elegant boxes (and shoeboxes) and neatly organized (and not so organized) albums. They hold tangible reminders of moments I want never to forget. During my thirty years as a high school teacher, I have also stored up another collection of images that will never make their way to my photo boxes or albums; they have been captured not on film but in my mind and in my heart.

Alexi comes in late again. He hates clocks and schedules. He hates rules and assignments. But he likes me, so he is only ten minutes late . . . on most days. Today a music box is playing "Twinkle, Twinkle, Little Star" in his pocket, and as he peels a banana and drops his knapsack, he tells me he has written some things.

Alexi will write only on scraps of paper I give him. He seems to feel that his thoughts fit nicely on long, slim, ripped pieces in the many colors I have salvaged. Today, in his completely dysgraphic way, he writes of churches and boxes and pieces of twine and fake faces melting in the snow. He writes that all these things are the same and wants to know if I agree, or at least see. He wants to know if what he has written is a poem. That is only one strip of paper.

He has filled an artist's sketchbook with pictures but refuses to keep a writer's notebook of images cast in words. He is himself a sight to note: half high on caffeine, half asleep, big silver earrings, almost Rasta hair. His mother is only fourteen years older than he is. His father is long gone, after saying one day to Alexi, "You are not my son." Now, Alexi is in my class, mine now, since being let out of psychiatric lockup after four years of being angry. I have no paperwork on him; I just have him. Yet, when he asks for scissors and glue and gets out a razor, I somehow know he will use them only to work in some new way with paper and markers, creating another kind of picture of his own. *Snap.*

Tom peeks in, on his way to someone else's class. His head is mowed in uneven strips with only a little eye makeup on today. He hands me something. "Here," he says. "I thought you might want your own fake blood capsule." I assure him I do, and as the next bell rings, he leaves. *Snap.*

Just before our test on *Catcher in the Rye*, after our class has spent days trying to figure out what it is that Holden needs to survive, Heaven comes up and asks me for a Band-Aid. She shows me her palm with two blisters. She wants me to know how hard it is twirling a flag for the band front. She likes my Band-Aids, which are cool Day-Glo orange and neon green with sea horses and stars all over them. These are juniors in high school, and I see a line forming. All the girls are making up booboos because they like my Band-Aids. The boys are hacking so that I will give them cough drops from my jar, because they are hungry and this period is just before lunch. They need so much attention. *Snap.*

During lunch Jay finds me with half a tuna sandwich sticking out of my mouth. He wears the uniform of the United States Marines. He wants to show me what a man he has become in the year since I have seen him. He tells me how many pushups he can do and then tells me the Marine name for all the objects in my room.

"We call the window the 'porthole,' and that pole is a 'stanchion,'" he says.

The next day we join NATO in sending troops to Bosnia. *Snap.*

In the block after lunch, Josh falls asleep while everyone else in this senior class is doing information searches about Vietnam. They are ignoring him. I do, too, until I see that, openmouthed, he has actually begun to drool from the desk down to the floor. Mean, mouthy Rich has started to notice. Time to wake up Josh and remind him of his promise to do his work so he can qualify for basketball. The "things they carried" in author Tim O'Brien's Vietnam do not interest Josh, and he does not know from Bosnia. *Snap.*

The staff of the literary magazine comes in. Sara wears a blue stick-um star on her cheek and glitter on her eyelids, like star dust. I love the way she sparkles, both the girl and her writing. Meanwhile, Katie, using a blunt eyebrow pencil, has drawn a big flower around one of her eyes with leaves and tendrils looping down one side of her face. She plays the harmonica outside my classroom, but when the bell rings, she sits down to write about daggers and revenge. *Snap.*

Raub has shaved off all his hair except for one tuft. There is a scab where he pressed too hard. He looks like Zippy the Pinhead. Today he wears what looks like radioactive protective gear, a silver jacket and silver pants. Yesterday it was a lemon yellow sheath dress over brown corduroy pants. While many students torment each other over differences, Raub shrugs it off and never stoops to make a nasty remark about another living soul. He does, however, as usual, have a wild, one-sentence, thirty-second, breathless story to tell me before he can settle down to work. *Snap.*

I am sitting in the computer lab during the last block of the day, and the teacher-who-ditches-students has sent a dozen down to me. Noel is happy I am there. His twin brother, Gunnar, is in a class of mine, and Noel wants me to know that he is a writer, too. He types and then nudges me. "What do you think of this?"

He says he brought a story for me. It is in his locker. Can he go get it? He wants me to know that his brother is not always as nice as the teachers seem to think. He wants me to know that when he and his twin were six, Gunnar tried to poison him by putting something awful in his macaroni and cheese. *Snap.*

A new student comes up to me at the end of the day with a photograph album. "This is my mother," she says, opening her plastic book. She shows me her mother in a hospital bed with tubes in her nose. She died of AIDS.

"This is my sister. She is in Mrs. Hobart's class. Maybe you remember her from study hall last year?

She says she knows you.

"This is one of my foster mothers.

"This is my cousin and her baby. My cousin is fifteen. She is so lucky. I can't wait to have a baby.

"Here is a picture of my father. He sent it to me. I never met him, but I am going to see him someday.

"Look at the nice Christmas tree we had last year.

"This is where I live now. My sister lives there, too, so I like it.

"Do you still publish students' poetry for the school? See here? I wrote this about my mother. It rhymes and it's short. Do you think you could put it in the magazine?"

She picks up the album and hugs it, staring at me until I say, "Yes, of course. Of course I will publish your poem." *Snap.*

Every day I add more pictures. The boxes are overflowing, the albums bulge, and the walls are covered. Somehow, I always find room for more, and there is always space in my mind and in my heart. *Snap.*

—*Beverly Carol Lucey*

What Teaching Justin Taught Me

The first time I met Justin, his face twisted with red rage. After years of public school teaching, it takes a lot to unsettle me, but when Justin strode into my room, tossed his flimsy notebook on the desk, and defiantly put his feet up on the table, I froze. I had known him exactly three seconds, and he was already being insolent to my authority.

I politely asked Justin to remove his muddy feet from the furniture and carefully mentioned that there was an assignment on the board.

"I ain't got no pen," he spat.

I was ready to launch into my "how old are you, and can't you bring a pen to class" lecture when it occurred to me that he must be at least twenty years old. As a vocational school teacher, I often see older students, but Justin possessed a terrified-little-boy quality wrapped up in a man's body. His face was weathered and pockmarked with bright red acne. He wore a dirty plaid shirt over torn, mud-caked jeans ripped at the hem and written on with green marker. His shoes were untied, and his brown socks slumped at his ankles.

Everything about Justin suggested trouble-maker—including, and except for, his eyes. A steely blue, they pierced through me with a warning glare. Yet, those same crystal-clear blue eyes, like deep pools of water, are what made me quietly place my own pen on his desk and walk away. It was a small gesture of armistice to let him know I wasn't the enemy. I thought it might allow him to drop his guard a bit, but he had already decided to hate me. He leisurely opened his notebook and began writing. I sighed and continued walking the aisles, glancing back toward Justin with the softest smile I could muster.

It had taken five hard years of teaching for me to learn which battles to pick on the first day of class. Not being prepared for class was a battle for the second day. I knew a few things, but Justin taught me many new lessons over the course of our eighteen weeks together. I struggled to help him improve his writing with the goal in mind that he might be able to complete a job application. He lacked basic skills of every kind; he didn't capitalize the first word in sentences, and he wrote as if he had never heard of punctuation. He struggled to contain his constantly boiling anger, but it was so bottled up that some days the cork burst and pelted whoever was near. The other students learned to avoid Justin, and the seats on either side of him were always empty. He acted as if his social leprosy didn't bother him and took his space as an invitation to lounge his limbs on the vacant seats.

Usually, his rage was directed at an inanimate object, a chair or one of my computers. "I hate these stupid things, and they hate me," he would shout. I would quickly join Justin at his workstation and instruct him how to work through the printing problem or how to access his work on the school's server. I had taught him these simple tasks a dozen times, but Justin could never retain the knowledge and every day was a trial of patience for both of us.

I knew that answering his rage with anger would only escalate an argument to a dangerous level. The day his fury finally erupted at me was one of the most frightening of my teaching career. I was seated at a work table conferencing quietly with two students who had peer edited each other's essays. "Your thesis is strong, and I like the way you organized the conclusion," I counseled, "Maybe you should . . . " My voice trailed off as I saw Justin out of the corner of my eye kick the computer table.

Without turning my face, I called in his direction, "Justin, move your chair away from the computer and count to ten. I will be there to help you soon."

Assuring Justin in this way typically bought me some time until I could finish working with another student. I was always careful not to immediately drop what I was doing and race to Justin's side, fearing that would simply reward his impatience and send the message that his fury was justified. Just as I was resuming my conference, Justin let loose.

"I can't do any of this, and it's your fault, Mrs. Young!"

He flung the contents of the table in my direction. I stared at the papers at my feet, hoping his tirade would end. Justin repeatedly kicked the tower of the computer, crumpling the metal. He stormed from the room, tears of fury glistening in his eyes.

Silence descended as all eyes watched to see what I would do next. The tension was as thick as soup. I was actually thankful that Justin had left, because it avoided the scene of kicking him out or having him removed for his behavior. I knew that his outburst had gone too far. This time, I would not be able to coax him through his anger or listen while he lamented all the things that went wrong in his life. I walked casually to the door, trying to calm my beating heart. The hallway was as empty as a tomb. I telephoned the dean's office to let them know that he was loose. Then I closed my classroom door and resumed class. Though my pulse was racing, I wanted to reassure my students that the situation was under control.

When the bell rang I took to the hallways looking for Justin. I wasn't sure what I would say, but I knew that his punishment would be out of my hands. His discipline record at our school was already thick with pink slips, and I knew that he was on the verge of expulsion. He had already been expelled from any other place he might be able to go, including the trailer he shared with his aunt and her four children. Justin had backed himself into a tight corner with no clear exits.

During my next two class periods, I heard his name called repeatedly over the intercom. When the bell finally rang for lunch, I decided to check the bathrooms one last time. As I called into the boys' restroom, I heard a strange scratching sound coming from the carpentry class next door. The building was supposed to be empty, as the lunchroom is across campus, so I quietly opened the shop door.

There was Justin, furiously sanding away at the leg of a table. He didn't see me at first, and I watched as he slid his hand gracefully over the surface, checking its smoothness. When he finished sanding, he reached for the clear stain and the paintbrush and noticed my presence. He hesitated for a moment, but then continued his work without saying a word. It was then that I noticed the table and its design. The wood was a marbled red pine with carefully carved edges. The surface had been masterfully engraved with a rose pattern and the legs finished in a powerful yet delicate claw. It was a gorgeous piece of furniture, and the skill and labor put into it were evident.

"Justin, that is exquisite!" I exclaimed, forgetting my anger.

He bowed his head and shrugged. "I just want to finish it before I leave," he mumbled.

My heart sank as I lowered myself to the floor to watch. We both checked the clock to see how much time until the next bell, when our secret would be revealed. Punishment was the last thing on my mind. I felt hopeless to help Justin, knowing the hole he had dug was his own. But as I watched him work, a feeling of hope for this young man washed over me. I chided myself for dismissing his abilities and judging him to be handicapped simply because he couldn't write complete sentences. Justin had a gift. If only he could channel his talent and couple it with some self-control, he could achieve something remarkable or at least support himself and his family.

I don't know where Justin is today. He left the carpentry class before the final coat of stain he'd so carefully applied to the table had dried. I think of him often and sometimes imagine him as an apprentice in a cabinetry or furniture shop somewhere, working away at another masterpiece in an environment where he has better outlets for his emotions and more support for his ambitions. I think of what he taught me about judging people too quickly. I don't know whether the patience I showed Justin gave him an example of an alternative way of being. I hope so. Sometimes, though, I feel that the baggage students come in with is just too heavy to unpack. But as I sit back in my classroom and admire his beautiful table in front of me, I am reminded that we all have value.

—Melissa Scholes Young

Flight Dreams

M
r. Zumstein and I both wanted to fly in
space. He hoped to hitch a ride on the
space shuttle as a teacher; I dreamed of becoming a
full-fledged astronaut. Never mind that the probability
of my middle-aged high school science teacher's being
accepted into NASA's Teacher-in-Space program was
about as high as that of my science-challenged brain
scoring an A in his chemistry and physics classes. The
odds didn't deter either of us.

"I'm still having trouble with those study problems you gave us yesterday for the test," I told Mr.
Zumstein at one of my 7:15 A.M. tutoring sessions.

I removed the page out of my cluttered book bag
and showed him my notes. He looked it over, nod-
ding his head. With a pencil, he scratched a few
modifications to my theorems and handed the page
back to me.

"You'll get it," he said. "Keep practicing."

Mr. Zumstein and I enjoyed an easy camaraderie, despite our differences. He was a mild-mannered veteran of the teaching corps, a master of the sciences in all but biology at Tremont High. I was an outgoing teenage girl who excelled in English, speech, and band. Our school numbered about three hundred students, large enough to keep aloof from your teachers if you worked at it, but small enough to become friends with them if you had something in common. Mr. Zumstein and I followed the space program. While my dreams remained youthfully optimistic and open-ended, his hopes had been tempered by an eventual rejection letter from NASA, thanking him for his application and his interest in the program.

"What an opportunity that will be for somebody," he said, shrugging his shoulders. "Maybe next time."

I might have been young, but I understood that in order to become an astronaut, I needed to improve my lackluster math and science skills. My nearsightedness knocked me off the pilot list, but I thought perhaps I could be a mission specialist or the first "writer in space," or maybe I could do public relations for NASA. All required a better grasp of math and science.

Mr. Zumstein shared in my enthusiasm and

recognized my deficiencies. He spent hours trying to teach my creative brain to think in a more logical manner. He helped me with algebra and geometry equations, chemistry and physics problems, and physical science experiments. He patiently explained principles, theorems, and rules over and again, tirelessly.

"You have to keep working the problems," he would say. "Eventually this will get easier for you."

I wanted to believe him, to believe that I could do anything I dreamed of.

Nonetheless, I struggled through algebra, taking it twice in an effort to understand and improve my grade. I took every imaginable science class: biology, physical science, chemistry, and physics. The Cs I earned in those classes dropped my grade point average, but I persevered, determined to overcome my ineptitude.

After my tutoring sessions, Mr. Zumstein and I talked about the constellations and planets I had observed through my telescope at home. We debated the merits of the space program, the challenges it faced to keep on schedule, and the pressures it encountered from the nonscience community.

"I heard on the radio that they delayed the shuttle launch again," I said one morning.

"I heard that, too. It's been one thing after another with this one." He shook his head. "Hopefully, they will take care of the problem and launch later this week."

"I don't understand why they can't get it right," I said. "The delays are brutal for the program."

I was looking at it from a personal perspective. If NASA was struggling, they would hire fewer people, decreasing my chances of working for them after college.

My frustrations with the space program's delays disappeared one cold day in January 1986, instantly replaced with shock. I was walking alone in the high school hallway, headed for the restroom, when our principal came over the loudspeaker:

"This morning, the space shuttle *Challenger* launched with a seven-member crew, including Christa McAuliffe, the first teacher in space. It is with great sadness that I have to tell you this: The shuttle was lost after approximately one minute of flight. It exploded, and all onboard are feared dead."

Suddenly sick to my stomach, I stopped where I stood. Surely, it couldn't be true. It was too terrible to be true. I felt sick to my stomach and leaned against a locker for support.

Mr. Zumstein had wheeled a television into his classroom to watch the coverage of the *Challenger*'s launch. Because I had a test in another class that period, I couldn't share with him the historic moment we both had been waiting for—the first teacher launched into space.

My heart ached for Mr. Zumstein. While I

dreamed of someday riding on a space shuttle, he had more than dreamed about it: He had actually applied to the program that had put a teacher on *this* space shuttle, the *Challenger*.

I went to his classroom and knocked on the door-frame. The television remained on, replaying the scene—the brilliant blue sky, the perfectly executed launch, the confused faces of the families as they watched the shuttle explode, mere seconds after NASA command said, "*Challenger*, go at throttle up."

My teacher turned toward me, his face downcast. He looked tired and a little older somehow. I hugged him, and we watched the TV for a few minutes more as the media speculated about the cause of the catastrophe.

"Launch is always the most dangerous time," he said. "The smallest mistake can have the worst of consequences."

I wondered aloud how the accident would impact NASA and the future of manned space flight, what the next few weeks and months would hold, and whether the exploration of space was worth the ultimate sacrifices of the *Challenger* crew.

"I'd go up tomorrow if they'd let me," Mr. Zum-stein said resolutely.

In the months that followed, Mr. Zumstein and I talked regularly throughout the *Challenger* investiga-tion. We rolled our eyes at the bureaucratic snafus and groaned at the simplicity of the O-ring culprit.

I kept at the algebra and chemistry lessons, all the time hoping NASA would regroup. Mr. Zumstein continued to teach his classes, tutoring those of us who still grappled with his subjects. He brought the television back into his classroom for the NCAA basketball tournament, maintaining his annual tradition of rooting for Duke, his alma mater.

Eventually, I graduated and moved on to a liberal arts university, where I pursued political science and communications. In a class on organizational structure, we studied a model of the *Challenger* disaster, but beyond that, I gave little thought to the space program during my college career. After graduating, I never did apply to NASA. By then, my interests were focused on politics and government.

Mr. Zumstein retired from the high school and moved into math and science instruction at a local community college. We exchanged Christmas cards and occasional e-mails.

Sixteen years after the *Challenger*, CNN reported that Barbara Morgan, Christa McAuliffe's backup all those years ago, would fly as the next teacher in space. Watching the news broadcast from my treadmill, I remembered my hope of one day rocketing into space. I thought of Mr. Zumstein and smiled. What a great supporter he had been of my dreams back then, knowing the whole time that I would probably never attain the skills I needed to enter the astronaut corps, but sticking with me anyway.

Several months later, I watched the memorial service for the *Columbia* astronauts from that same treadmill. Tears mixed with sweat streamed down my face, and I felt a familiar ache in my stomach. Then, I recalled what Mr. Zumstein had said all those years ago:

"I'd go up tomorrow."

And I knew he still would.

With those words, he had given me his most important lesson, better than any chemistry table or algebra equation: Some dreams are worth keeping, even for a lifetime.

—*Julie A. Kaiser*

What I Never Learned in Kindergarten

My kindergarten classroom was located on the left side of a hallway at the end of a corridor in a school so small it held only five classrooms. I was afraid of everything. I was afraid of not being able to open the large front door, the science experiments we sometimes did, and, most of all, my teacher.

Mrs. Monestel never smiled. She was old, wrinkled, and overweight. She frequently said, "That makes me very cross," with a deep scowl. In my memory, she always wore the same dress.

I remember very little else of my time in kindergarten, except that we read *Weekly Readers* and one of the boys kept coming out of the in-class bathroom with his pants down.

During a conference, Mrs. Monestel told my mother that, unfortunately, I was a very average child. I don't remember her acting as if anyone else in the class was particularly special, either. In the current debate about teachers who overinflate their students' self-esteem, Mrs. Monestel would have been championed by those who believe we are now overdoing it. I think that Mrs. Monestel didn't realize that, however small her students were, they were capable of having important moments.

My son's kindergarten teacher couldn't have been more different. At the end of Jeremy's kindergarten year, I went to see him perform in his class puppet show. I arrived early and admired the classroom. Projects were displayed all over the place. There was a chick-hatching project, a number of reading readiness projects, a book corner for those who were already readers, and a self-portrait project. There was a block corner, a few computers, clusters of desks and chairs where the children worked, mailboxes for the children, and a chart showing the weather. The room was exciting and warm at the same time, an inviting world for hungry minds.

First, I looked over all of Jeremy's work. Then I took my seat, my father's video camera in hand, in the rows of chairs that had been set aside for the parents to watch the puppet show. I had made an error regarding the time of the show and so had an opportunity not usually afforded those of us who are perpetually tardy: I had a preshow adventure.

Mrs. Feldheim was Jeremy's kindergarten teacher. She was rather petite and dressed in a very casual manner. She wore slightly Bohemian earrings and a smile. Never saccharine, she was always warm. She was walking around her classroom interacting with her students at work when there was a knock at the door.

"Mrs. Feldheim, may I come in?" a little boy asked tentatively.

"Oh, Paul, of course." Mrs. Feldheim bounded toward the door. Then she introduced the visitor. "Class, Paul has come here on a very special assignment today."

Paul's shoulders relaxed.

"He's in the second grade, you know."

Mrs. Feldheim's class grew quieter.

"He has chosen our class for his project. He's going to interview us about what it's like to spend a day in our kindergarten class. Let's all sit on the carpet."

Paul, whose head barely reached Mrs. Feldheim's hips, walked next to her. He was holding one of those thick pencils for kids who have just learned to write. His palms had pencil lead all over them. His well-bitten fingernails were also nearly black. He carried a tablet of extra-wide lined paper. Paul was a man on a mission.

Mrs. Feldheim's class went to the corner, where they had a brown, fuzzy carpet for their daily meetings, the kindergarten equivalent of a conference table. Once they were settled, the interview began. Paul stood beside Mrs. Feldheim, poised to ask his first question. The children were unusually quiet. Highly amused, I thought I wasn't going to be able to keep myself together. But Mrs. Feldheim took the matter entirely to heart.

"Paul, how would you like to conduct this interview? Would you like to ask one question to each student? How would that be?"

Paul appeared to be feeling terribly grand now. He had his pad and pencil ready to go, and he nodded that Mrs. Feldheim's suggestion was a good one.

"What is the first thing you do when you come in the room?" he asked the first little girl.

"Hang up my coat." She thought a bit more. "Well, only if it's cold outside."

Very slowly, Paul wrote down her response. He had to sit down, because he couldn't write in a standing position. I had been wondering if he could write at all.

"Good answer, Casey," said Mrs. Feldheim, and Casey beamed.

Now comfortably seated, Paul pointed to the next little girl. He was getting the hang of it. "What is your favorite activity?"

"Well, if someone is having a birthday, then that's it. But if not, maybe it's the weather report part."

"Ana, great answer," said Mrs. Feldheim, "very thoughtful."

Once again, Paul was busy writing. I could hardly contain myself. Paul couldn't have felt more important if he had been a cub reporter for the *New York Times*.

One by one, he quizzed the children. He wrote furiously and flipped pages as his notes grew longer. Occasionally, he would say something like, "Just give me a minute to finish here."

It was all I could do not to laugh. But Mrs. Feldheim wasn't laughing. Given the expression on her face, what was going on might well have had a profound effect on our national security.

As Paul's interview continued, the children grew more interested and their answers became more thoughtful. I think Paul even ad-libbed a few questions by virtue of his having been a student of Mrs. Feldheim's two years earlier. Finally, he completed his task. He looked plainly exhausted. All of that writing had used up his entire tablet and most of his strength. But he was proud. Mrs. Feldheim's class had remained attentive to the end, which was remarkable.

Paul stood up, and Mrs. Feldheim shook his dirty little hand. Her expression remained earnest. "Paul, thank you so much for choosing our class for your interview," she said, as though he'd had a wide range of venues from which to choose. As Paul began to leave, she said, "Oh, Paul? If you write it up, I would really appreciate it if you could make me a copy for my files."

I don't know if Paul was ever able to compile a meaningful piece of writing from his notes, and it is even more doubtful that Mrs. Feldheim ever received a copy of it, but after the puppet show, which was its own wonderful experience, I began thinking about Mrs. Feldheim. I realized that her response to Paul's assignment was the reason she is a teacher and I am not. Something that I saw as comical, she took seriously. She took what could have been a routine exchange and created several moments of personal history, not only for Paul, but for all the students in her class.

I eventually came to know "Mrs. Feldheim" as "Naomi." In a gesture that I found flattering, she invited me to dinner after Jeremy graduated kindergarten. As for Paul, our budding journalist, I don't know what became of him. I suppose he's applying to college now. One thing for sure, he and my son were lucky they didn't have to suffer with the very cross Mrs. Monestel.

—*Debbi Klopman*

The Gift

One morning my oldest daughter, Rhonda, rushed in my front door. "Mom, the most wonderful thing just happened."

I smiled, remembering Rhonda's enthusiasm as a young girl, when she would come barreling into our home with news of her day. Now, as a wife and mother of two, she could still energize a room.

"Good morning, Rhonda, and a good morning to you too, sweet pea," I said, picking up my two-year-old granddaughter. "Let's sit and have coffee and cookies. Then you can tell me all about your news." Turning around, I looked at my daughter. "Are you pregnant?"

"No, Mom," Rhonda answered. Sitting with her coffee cup in hand, she sighed with excitement. "Mrs. Perkins, the director of Saint Francis School, told me this morning that an anonymous person is paying Greg's tuition. Mom, they're paying his tuition for the whole year."

Rhonda's eyes filled with tears as she grabbed my hand. "Was it you, Mom? You and Dad?"

"No, I wish we could, but it wasn't us," I said.

Rhonda and her husband, Gil, had both selected the role of educators for their careers. I remembered when, as newlyweds, they set off for their first teaching jobs, ready to change the world, one child at a time, if necessary.

After Rebekah was born, Rhonda and Gil decided to tighten their belts and live on one income. Rhonda gave up her paid teaching job and became a full-time, stay-at-home mom, reserving her teaching for her own little ones.

This was great for their children but hard on their pocketbook. Greg showed signs of being a gifted child and could read at the age of three. Rhonda and Gil talked at length and decided to send him to a private preschool for two days a week. The school was expensive, but it offered great teachers with small classrooms and produced good results. Knowing they would have difficulty paying the tuition alone, they had requested a partial scholarship. The director assured them this was a common practice and that they had several alums who helped out from time to time. No one had dreamed someone would pay the whole amount of Greg's tuition.

Rhonda, still holding the note from the school in her hand, said. "I just wish I knew who was so generous."

"Rhonda, I think that, whoever the benefactor is, it must be important to them to keep their identity private." Giving her a hug, I continued, "Count your blessings. And someday you can do the same for someone else."

"Mom, you're such a Pollyanna! But I sure would like to know. That's a lot of money. I wrote a thank-you note and asked Mrs. Perkins to see that the donor receives it."

Several months later, near the end of the school year, Rhonda was dropping Rebekah off at my house to spend a couple of hours while she ran some quick errands. We said our good-byes as Rhonda hunted through her purse for her misplaced keys.

"Shoot, I forgot to sign and return this," she said, retrieving an envelope. Greg had brought home a permission slip to attend a field trip. When she opened the envelope, a small piece of pink paper fell to the floor.

"What's this?" I asked, picking up the paper and handing it to Rhonda.

Rhonda scanned the paper. "Mom, look," she said as tears rolled down her face. "It was Christie, Christie Leeks. Someone in the Saint Francis office must have put this receipt in Greg's envelope by mistake." Christie was making monthly payments of $120 for Greg's tuition.

Christie Leeks was a young girl who had been in Rhonda's first dance class at the high school where she had taught five years earlier. Christie had lived in the Methodist Home as a ward of the state. Rhonda and Gil had taken Christie and another student who lived at the foster home under their wings. They invited them to their home for Sunday dinners, baked them birthday cakes, counseled and loved them. After two years, Rhonda and Gil moved to another city and new jobs. They lost contact with the other student, who had moved out of the country, but stayed in touch with Christie over the years. Rhonda and Gil even traveled back to attend Christie's high school graduation and then helped her move into a college dorm.

"How can she pay for this?" Rhonda asked. "This has to be a hardship on her; I know she is only making student wages. We can't accept this. I have to call her and tell her to stop."

"Rhonda, it's obviously important to Christie for you not to know. You can't tell her you found out her secret."

A few months later, during Greg's summer vacation from school, Christie stopped by to visit and celebrate a belated birthday. That night, Rhonda and Christie sat up talking, while the rest of the household slept. Christie, about to graduate from college with honors, had met a special young man.

"I am so proud of you, Christie," Rhonda said. "You have grown into a special young woman. I always knew you would, from the first day I saw you in class."

"Mrs. Davidson, I want to show you something," Christie said as she went to her overnight bag and retrieved her Bible. Opening it, she removed the thank-you note Rhonda and Gil had written to the anonymous contributor. "Would you read this, Mrs. Davidson?"

As Rhonda read the note aloud, she had to swallow the lump in her throat.

Rhonda read the last sentence. . . .

> We only hope that one day we can give to a child as you have so generously given to our child.

"Don't you know, Mrs. Davidson? I am that child. You and Mr. Davidson taught me and gave me so much. This was a small way I could say 'Thank you.'"

I often reflect on this rewarding experience in my daughter's life and on Christie's generosity. I think of all the other students whose lives have been positively impacted by Rhonda and Gil, in ways these two young teachers will never know. With Christie, they were fortunate. Not only did they get to see the positive outcome of the life they touched, but they also saw their gift of compassion returned to them.

—Hattie Mae Ratliff

Ant Bites

"Ow! Ow!" I shouted as I broke my jump rope rhythm and tangled my feet in the slack rope. "Something in my shoe is biting me," I wailed.

The first graders waiting to jump and the two rope turners circled around me on the dirt playground. My teacher, Miss Bell, heard me and hurried over, leaving the other recess teacher in mid-conversation.

"It's still stinging me," I cried as the circle of children opened for Miss Bell.

"Which foot is it?" she asked.

I stuck up my right foot as she stooped over to inspect it. Just then, feeling a new sting, I yelped in pain.

"Here. Let's take off your shoe," instructed Miss Bell, squatting down to get the shoe.

Then, I remembered the holes in my socks.

Welfare socks didn't last long. Holes in socks were a common thing for our family in the years following the Great Depression. Shoes got fresh paper inserted every Saturday to cover the holes in their soles. But socks with holes were just accepted. Socks with holes in the heels got pulled down so the hole wouldn't show. Where there was a hole, there would soon be a blister. Every week as she washed our clothes, Mama would say, "Even if we're poor and our clothes are worn out, we can still be clean."

I began to cry from the pain in my foot, but I refused to let Miss Bell take off my shoe. I could not bear for her and the others to see the hole in my faded red sock.

"Come on, then. Let's go inside to the office."

A trail of first graders followed after us until Miss Bell told them to stay on the playground. I did my best to curb my tears. Yet, each time the thing in my shoe stung me, I would let out a loud, "Oh, oh, oh!" Tears raced down my contorted face.

Mr. Stewart, the principal, rushed into his office. "What's wrong?" he asked.

"Something is stinging her right foot, but she will not let me take off her shoe," said Miss Bell.

Mr. Stewart lifted me onto his desk. "Let me take a look." He just about had the shoe off when I saw the hole. I grabbed the shoe and pulled it on and held it. The stinging worsened the tighter I clasped the shoe.

"Why won't you let us take off your shoe?" Mr. Stewart asked as he looked from me to Miss Bell and back at me in puzzlement.

Miss Womble, the fifth-grade teacher, came into the office. "Can I help? I know her; she lives next door to me."

"I suspect ants are in her shoes and stinging the living daylights out of her, but she won't let us take off her shoes," related Miss Bell.

Miss Womble was a great neighbor. She had even played Annie-over with us on occasion. She put both hands on my shaking shoulders and looked into my distressed, red eyes.

"Oh, yes," she said, as if remembering a fact. "I had a bite from one of those ants. Did you know they are sock eaters? By the time I got my shoe off, that ant had eaten almost the entire bottom off my sock." She nodded her head up and down as she looked at the other two adults. "Must be sock-eater ants."

They returned the nod, as if they, too, had been bitten by sock-eating ants.

"Let me see here." She freed my heel from the shoe. "Just what I thought. Those sock ants have eaten part of her sock."

Miss Bell opened the medicine cabinet, got a cotton ball, and saturated it with alcohol. Miss Womble slipped off my shoe and sock and shook both of them over the gray trash bucket. Two red ants fell into the waiting container. A stray one ran for the wall, but Mr. Stewart's shoe stopped him.

My swollen foot throbbed. My stomach hurt. My head ached.

Stroking the alcohol ball across the angry bites, Miss Womble lifted her head and smiled at me. "I think she's going to be okay now," she said, as she glanced toward the two adults.

The bell rang, ending the recess period. "It's class time," Mr. Stewart remarked, as he and Miss Bell hurried to their duties.

The alcohol felt cool on the savage welts.

"You were a pretty brave girl to take that many bites. I think you should leave this shoe and sock off for awhile." She helped me off the desk. "Wait for me after school, and we'll walk home together."

Pride can be a wonderful, terrible thing. I knew that Miss Womble had saved my pride with her sock-eating ant story. She had seen that I would rather be stung to death than to let others see my poverty. This kind, insightful teacher had taught me a lesson of compassion that I have tried to apply in my thirty-seven years of teaching.

—*Emmarie Lehnick*

From Intro to Coda

Sometimes being a "special" teacher isn't all that special. You know what I mean. How many times have we had to deal with inflexible schedules, those who think we have it easy, the idea that we are not "real" teachers teaching a "real" subject? We teachers of music and art and drama and such get the remains—leftover classroom space (if we're lucky enough to get off the cart or out of the all purpose/no purpose room), furniture, rehearsal time—and whatever scrapings are left at the bottom of the budget. We are constantly fending off the parent who doesn't understand why Billy or Susie gets homework or a grade in music, trying to stretch ourselves between hundreds of students at several different schools, and coping with a chronic lack of equipment. Some days, it is enough to make us second-guess our decisions to teach these "special" subjects.

Despite the relentless testing of my fortitude, if given the chance, I probably would still choose to be a music teacher. Because, you see, being a special teacher puts me in a special position. Every now and then there are those special times—the moments when I realize the impact I've had on a student. As an extra added bonus, I am able to see my students grow from virtual babies to mature adolescents. I watch them develop from apprehensive five- and six-year-olds to secure second and third graders. I see them change from fun-loving fourth and fifth graders to wary sixth- and seventh-grade students. Then, almost magically, they transform into poised eighth-grade graduates. From there I can only imagine the adventures that await them. Some will fulfill their dreams; others will not. Some successes I will learn of; others will go unspoken.

Take Owen, for example. When he was in eighth grade, my spring show had a back-to-the-fifties theme. I needed a soloist for "Love Me Tender." Having no volunteers, I began to recruit. Owen was reluctant, but with the help of some encouraging classmates, I persuaded him to sing. He had never done anything like that before; it would be his debut. The show was a smashing success, with Owen in his leather jacket, girls swooning, and thunderous applause. Ah, a success story, but the story doesn't end there.

Several years later while teaching at another

school, I was arranging an end-of-the-year outing for my grades four through eight choir. We were planning a trip to the local high school for their production of *The King and I*. Much to my surprise, Owen was cast in the title role. There he was on stage, mature and full of confidence, not at all the shy guy who sang the eighth-grade solo. My heart was filled with so much pride, you'd have thought I had given birth to him. In a way, maybe I had.

Then there is John. I had been John's general music teacher since kindergarten. He was a precocious child, mature beyond his years. It was obvious early on that he had a gift. By sixth grade he was accompanying my choir; by eighth grade he was better than some adults. He could play anything I threw at him. Once he bailed me out by accompanying my spring show when my scheduled pianist cancelled at the last minute.

I cried the night John's mother called to tell me he had won the piano solo competition for the annual archdiocesan festival. Consequently, this high school senior was to perform Liszt on stage at the Academy of Music in Philadelphia, and he wanted me to be among the first to know and to invite me to attend. His performance was flawless, leaving me breathless. Again, my heart filled with joy, remembering the child I had once taught while witnessing the exceptional young man he had become.

I have seen the effect a music teacher can have on a student from the other side, as a parent, too. I observed this firsthand with my son, Charlie. I watched him change from a struggling fourth grader who sometimes felt academically inadequate compared to his peers into a self-assured saxophone player. His instrumental teacher believed in him and made him believe in himself, encouraging and gently pushing him to work to the best of his ability. He went on to perform in the high school marching band and jazz band. He had enough faith in himself to audition for and earn a drum major position while only in tenth grade. Then he set and achieved the goal of becoming Atlantic Coast Conference Best Drum Major.

In a card I received from Matt, a fifth-grade piano student, at the end of this school year, he wrote, "Thank you for a great year. I can't wait to see what is to come." Neither can I, because this year, after only two years of lessons, Matt accompanied the kindergarten at the spring show and played for their graduation, and he has begun to accompany the ensemble in church. I cannot wait to see what the next chapter in Matt's musical life brings.

Not all of our elementary and middle school students are destined for greatness in the performing arts arena. Yet, how many times have you seen them come alive in that special way that only self-discovery of a hidden talent can bring? Take my eighth-grade class this year. First, meet Danielle. She is an average student in a class of brainiacs. She is a hardworking student who is often overshadowed by the accomplishments of some of her classmates. Dani played the lead role in this year's play. She carefully memorized and executed every line, carrying herself like a pro on stage. You could see her transform with every rehearsal into a more confident young lady.

Meet Justin, a very serious student. I remember Justin being part of a first grade group dressed as brown paper-wrapped packages, singing "I'm Gonna Mail Myself to You." Now, there he was, mesmerizing the younger students with his portrayal of Harry Potter, complete with glasses and British accent. He allowed himself to be vulnerable, to sing and dance, to skip with the other characters on stage. His excitement sparked others to let go and have fun with their parts. He became a crowd favorite in the process.

I do not profess to be the most talented or innovative music teacher. I am just a humble warrior in the fight to keep the arts alive. I am sure you each have your own John, Owen, Dani, Justin, Charlie, and Matt. Each of us, as music teachers, is a keeper of the flame. Sometimes, it seems as though we are rubbing those sticks together forever before a fire ignites. Other times, we spark flash fires that seem to die out as quickly as they began. Just remember, though, that as long as we keep even a flicker of the fire alive, there is always a chance it will ignite the flames of music or drama or art in another student again.

We teachers of the arts are very lucky to be special. A "regular" teacher gets a student for a year—a mere movement. We, on the other hand, get to see the overture to the finale and hopefully an encore. So, on those days when we long to be regular, too, just remember how special being special really is.

—*Rita DiCarne*

Dial A for Effort

I teach English as a second language (ESL) to kids aged eleven to fifteen. My school is in Wisconsin. My students are from Mexico, Puerto Rico, Asia, and Africa, and they struggle daily to conquer both a new language and a new culture.

Though I absolutely love my job and eagerly look forward to talking with and teaching my students every day, I freely admit that it is not without its challenges and frustrations, including unmotivated and annoying students. On the other hand, there are always those few special kids who become my favorites. Although veteran teachers repeatedly warn against forming any personal attachments to students, in my opinion, it is simply not possible to avoid it. Sometimes, one of my favorites is also one of my greatest challenges—like Luis.

Luis is fourteen years old and moved here with his family from Mexico five years ago. His often smiling, honey-brown face is sprinkled with freckles, and his dark eyes reveal both innocence and wariness. Small and skinny, he has the slightly hunched shoulders of a beaten dog. When I place my hand on his back to encourage him, he always flinches slightly. Luis looks around carefully before he laughs, wanting to fit in. Yet, his hairstyle is quite distinctive—very short, almost shaved, except for a "rat tail" that hangs in the front, like a forgotten piece of bangs.

Having noticed the markings written on his notebooks, I am aware that Luis is being courted by a gang. It makes my throat tighten with distress to think of this sweet kid with dimples involved in life-threatening situations or acts of violence. Sadly, this is a reality many students live with daily.

From the beginning of the year, Luis attended school an average of two times a week. Consistently polite and friendly, he'd grown accustomed to blending into the background, where no one really noticed his absence. I did.

After a previous day of nonattendance, I inquired where he had been.

"At home."

"Why were you at home? You don't look sick."

"I don't know, Miss. I was just home," he said.

I reminded him that his grade was suffering in my

class and he had a lot of work to make up. He just nodded and looked repentant.

Finally, after a couple of weeks of continued absences with the same nonexplanation, I called his home. Speaking Spanish, I informed Luis's father that his son was missing too much school. The man told me he understood and would speak to Luis. I hung up the phone feeling a sense of accomplishment and satisfaction.

The next week, Luis made his standard two appearances.

Unwilling to give up on the little guy, I spent a good part of the weekend brainstorming what I should do and decided to appeal to his feelings. I have learned that my students do not want to disappoint me, neither as their teacher nor as a person who cares about them.

The following Monday morning, once again Luis did not show up. As the students took their seats and began the daily routine of copying the lesson from the board, I went over to the phone.

Luis answered, and I could hear a Spanish television show blaring in the background.

"What are you doing at home?" I demanded. "By the way, this is Ms. Ritchie."

He laughed weakly. "I am sick."

"You are not sick," I said firmly. "Don't even try that one on me. I do not appreciate you taking a vacation day. Class isn't the same when you're absent. I like it much better when you are here, and I expect to see you in class tomorrow. Understand?"

"I'll try, Miss."

"Don't 'Miss' me and then just 'try.' Be here! We miss you, Luis. See you tomorrow."

"Okay, Miss. Bye," he said quietly.

Meanwhile, the class had turned toward me and heard everything. When I hung up, they all said, "Miss, did you really call Luis at home? Is he skipping? He's skipping, isn't he, Miss?"

I smiled and said, "That, my dear students, is between Luis and me, but I thank you for your concern."

They laughed and started joking in Spanish that I was crazy and they couldn't believe I had called Luis and not his parents.

Luis showed up every day for the rest of the week. The next Monday arrived, and Luis was absent again. That week was especially important for the eighth graders to be in class, because they had grade-level assessments to pass if they wanted to graduate. And I had repeatedly stressed this point to all my students. So, while I took attendance that day, the kids all hollered, "Miss, Miss, Luis is skipping. Yeah, he is at home. He should be here, Miss. Are you going to call him? Are you? Are you? Ooooh . . . I wanna hear this!"

I smiled and motioned for them to turn around in their desks and mind their own business. Then I walked to the phone and dialed Luis's number.

This time, however, his mom answered. I introduced myself in Spanish and asked to speak to Luis. She sounded a bit surprised and called him to the phone.

He answered with a curious voice. "Hello?"

"Luis. What is your problem? You know that you must pass these tests or you'll be in eighth grade again next year. Though I would love to spend another year with you, it is time to move on to high school. And I do not appreciate you staying home for no good reason. If I have to, I will bring this test to your house, and, believe me, I will be annoyed if I have to do that. You do not get to fail my class. Either get yourself to school tomorrow, or I will show up at your house. Are we clear?" I said all this without pausing to let him get a word in edgewise.

I knew the entire class was listening attentively because the room was so quiet. But when I hung up the phone, the kids quickly turned back around in their seats, as if I hadn't noticed them eavesdropping. So I asked if they had heard the entire phone call.

"Yeah, Miss. We heard everything. What did he say? Are you really going to his house?"

Instead of answering, I asked for a show of hands if they believed I would actually do that, which for them was unheard-of teacher behavior. Every student's hand went up in the air.

One boy called out, "Yes, Miss. We know you are crazy like that. Luis will be here. Don't panic."

From that day on, I realized I must hold them accountable to me, because we care about each other. So, I don't let much slide by. When I notice a pattern of attendance or homework problems, I contact the parents first. If that doesn't change anything, I call and speak directly to the student. I want everyone to understand that the absence is personal to me and diminishes the class.

I knew this strategy was working when two different students called me during their usual class time to explain why they were at home. And in the past four months, Luis has missed only two days. Both of those days I called him to find out why, and he had a valid excuse. Plus, his attitude in the class has completely changed; he is attentive and works hard.

I believe that Luis wants and needs the attention and praise I dole out. I say things like, "See how smart you are to figure that out? You are going to fly right through high school and college." Then, he shines with pride, even though he has to maintain his "coolness" factor and shrugs it off.

Now, he stops in just to say hi between classes, and he doesn't flinch when I touch his back. I've said I intend to follow his progress with his high school teachers and that if I hear one word about him being in a gang or missing a lot of school, I will hunt him down just to yell at him. Luis just laughs.

The other day while he was working diligently at his desk, I knelt down next to him. "Luis, even when you are older and bigger and a tough guy," I said quietly near his ear, "I will still remember you as my sweet eighth grader with the crazy rat-tail hair who finally realized how smart he is. And surely you will remember me as the annoying teacher who called you at home to yell at you for skipping my class. I hope you also remember how much I believe in you and care about you."

He looked down, tucked the rat-tail hair behind his right ear and replied with a smile, "Yeah, Miss. I know."

—A. Ferreri

Pass It On

As the din of children's chattering and laughter disappeared down the hallway and the school buses roared out of the circle, in an otherwise empty classroom, two people worked quietly together—a young woman and a nine-year-old girl. I was the girl: a shy, overweight fourth grader with frizzy hair, glasses, and all the wrong unfashionable clothes, the type of student other kids bullied after school. Ms. Pinkham was my teacher, and what she taught me that year set off a chain reaction that would shape the course of my life . . . and take me full circle.

Ms. Pinkham could have attempted to boost my confidence with self-esteem pep talks or even tips on how to dress better, for I admired her pretty brown hair, which fell below her shoulders, and the stylish clothes she wore. She was a patient, imaginative, and thorough teacher, which ensured my academic development under her tutelage. She also recognized and encouraged my passion for reading and writing, which certainly endeared her to me. But Ms. Pinkham gave me something far more valuable than counsel, instruction, and praise: she gave me her time.

For most of fourth grade, I lingered in the classroom after school, doing little jobs for Ms. Pinkham. She let me cut out construction paper pumpkins for Halloween and hearts for Valentine's Day. I stapled scalloped boarders around the bulletin boards showcasing our spelling tests and book reports. We talked about the books we read and about cats (my favorite subject). In these little ways, Ms. Pinkham made a huge impression on me. Throughout grade school, high school, college, and grad school, I never forgot Ms. Pinkham's kindness. I found my niche in teaching college and began my career as a college professor filled with idealism. I would inspire my students with exciting books, stimulating discussions, and challenging writing assignments.

Before long, the real, hard world of teaching hit me like an avalanche.

The rain fell outside as I sat at my desk with a stack of papers before me. After just two years of teaching college English, I was exhausted. The long hours, overcrowded classes, and low pay overshadowed the enthusiasm I had once felt for teaching. I leaned over the first essay, written by a polite young man named Ben, and began to read. My eyes narrowed, and I went back and reread the first paragraph. The essay was written entirely in free verse poetry. The weird thing was that it was really good poetry and thoroughly covered the topic assigned. I paused, my pen hovering over Ben's poem. *How would I grade it? How could I teach him to write an academic paper but not lose his gift as a poet?*

My mind raced while the clock ticked. It was already growing late, and I had twenty-six more essays to go. I could have just inked a failing grade and a comment like "read the assignment." But I didn't. He didn't deserve a failing grade. And I remembered Ms. Pinkham, who probably could have gone home early many of those afternoons she'd stayed after with me. As the rain continued to fall and darkness crept over the room, I wrote notes in the margins of Ben's poem.

After I returned the essays to the students the following day, I found Ben standing by my desk at the end of class.

"Miz, " he began.

"Michele." I smiled as I gathered up my books.

"Miz . . . I mean, Michele," Ben continued. "I'm sorry about the essay. Can you help me with my next one?"

"Of course."

Ben actually didn't need much help. He just

needed a sounding board for his perspectives on life—his thoughts, dreams, and frustrations. The commentaries in the margins of the essays continued. In response, Ben wrote from his soul while learning and applying the formal structure of writing.

When the class ended, Ben and I remained friends. We shared our passion for American poets, Thoreau's *Walden,* and the fine art of river gazing. After receiving his bachelor's degree, Ben returned to college to earn his teaching credential.

One evening while I was working in my office, Ben stopped by to talk about his teaching classes.

"Most of my course work is great," he said. "But sometimes I feel like we are being taught to put students in boxes. Shouldn't we just let the children be themselves? Shouldn't we encourage that?"

I thought for a moment, and Ms. Pinkham came to mind. She hadn't tried to change me. She'd accepted and nurtured me.

"Yes," I agreed. "It isn't about boxes."

"It is about getting rid of the boxes to reveal the gifts inside," Ben said.

Ben went on to become a third-grade teacher, and he is amazing. Parents request their children to be in his class, and he just returned from a year of teaching the children of missionaries in Indonesia. Ben's passion for teaching inspires me.

I spend many hours preparing lesson plans and

lectures and many more bent over students' tests and essays, anxious to provide excellent guidance. Yet, I sometimes wonder whether I spend enough time with my students, whether I inspire them to love learning, whether I am an effective teacher. I may never know what, if any, impact I've had on many of my students, whose lives are connected with mine for only a short period. But when I see someone like Ben learn and grow, I realize that my greatest contribution to any student is my time.

I am positive that Ben will (if he hasn't already) make that connection with a student, just as Ms. Pinkham did with me. And with a genuine smile, a little extra time, encouraging words, or perhaps a few well-placed comments in the margin of an essay, he will inspire someone to take up the task of teaching others. Through simple acts of kindness, the teacher inspires the student who becomes the teacher who inspires the student, and so the cycle continues.

—*Michele Griskey*

Grieving the F

Jason slumped at his desk, chin on fist, staring at the paper in front of him. Several minutes earlier, I had given all the students computer printouts of their assignments and grades for the past month. The printouts, which detailed each student's cumulative performance in my sophomore English class, contained no surprises; all graded papers had been returned previously. The students accepted the records of their work with little comment, and when the bell rang they escaped in a burst of high spirits to lunch. Everyone, except Jason. As his friends headed out the door, they asked Jason if he was joining them. He just shook his head.

I looked at him, legs sprawled in the aisle, lock of long, auburn hair streaked with purple falling across one cheek, eyes downcast. *What about his printout could be troubling him?* He was a straight-A student.

He articulated original interpretations of the literature in class discussions and wrote with clarity and depth. He is one of those young people who light up the room and make me glad I teach. Jason shifted his weight, picked up the paper, set it down. He didn't look angry, just sad.

"What's wrong?" I asked. "Is there a mistake?"

"Only my mistake," he said. "I'm grieving my F. I didn't do a homework assignment."

It was hard to see him so unhappy. "Could you maybe celebrate the As?" I asked. "There are at least ten of them."

"No," he said simply. "Not yet. I have to grieve my F first."

He sat there a while longer. At last the sadness drained from his face, he nodded to me, smiled, and left.

Most students would say, "Hey, one assignment. No big deal." Not Jason. He went through a dark space before he could forgive himself.

A teacher to the core, I see a lesson in everything. Turning that incident over in my mind for days, I sensed this time the lesson was for me. But I hadn't a clue what it was and the image of Jason slumped at his desk faded.

Now, a decade later, I've been filling my luxurious days of retirement with ballroom dance. Last week I actually performed with a group of five couples. It wasn't a competitive event; we were just a little show at the intermission of a party for other dancers. Still, it was my first dance performance and I worried about it for a month. I wanted to wear black so the audience would notice me least among the ten dancers, but we were doing a Latin number and the women had to wear bright colors. *What if my mind went blank and I stood there in my sunflower yellow dress looking like a complete fool?*

We entered the room arm in arm with our partners. The audience, seated at tables along three walls, clapped. The music started. To my surprise, I smiled a genuine smile, danced with more style than I'd ever had, reveled in the spontaneous applause of the audience when we did an intricate step. I could do this. We got to the part of the dance where we changed partners. My second partner and I had never come together quite right, and I was a little afraid of him, besides.

Step-point, step-point, kick. Roll-through, cha-cha-cha, spot turn, pivot turn. And there I was, exactly in front of him. We started the next part of the routine. *Knee flex, syncopated cross-over.* I'd never dreamed I would do so well—until, abruptly, I had no idea where in the routine I was. My smile stayed pasted on my face, but my feet shuffled frantically. My partner strong-armed me through the next few moves, and eventually I found my place. I nailed the steps again. I snapped my head in the right places. We ended with a flourish and a deep bow.

Afterward, friends and strangers rushed to compliment the group, me included. I could hardly talk to them. *Hadn't my mistakes glowed in neon?* I talked to the other performers. Most of them had stumbled in at least one place, but they didn't care. They said there had been five couples to watch, so no one would notice one person's misstep. We'd been a grand success, and they'd had a good time. I tried to believe them and push away the ache of disappointment, to pretend I'd had fun, too.

But through the night, when I should have been sleeping, I mentally went over and over the place I hadn't done well, the music and the routine forming a continuous loop in my head. *I must not have practiced enough,* I scolded myself. *Or maybe I overpracticed.* Sometime in the early dawn, I remembered Jason—and got the lesson. I had rated my performance one F and ten A's, and I hadn't yet grieved my F. I got up, made a cup of warm milk, and attended to the pain of regret.

When I allowed myself to go down into it, my racing mind finally slowed. A memory of our sweeping entry and the audience's burst of applause flitted through my mind. *But you goofed,* my inner critic reminded me. *Yes, I certainly did,* I agreed. On the other hand, there was that friend's smile when I executed a snappy syncopation, the excellent transition. And the way I kept smiling when I lost my place till I got back on track. There was even the possibility I'd done better than I thought. Although my mind had quit working temporarily, my feet might have kept up with most of the steps. Over the next few days, I thought now and then of the place I had messed up. But more and more, I remembered that most of the dance had gone very well.

If I blank again next time I perform, I hope I will find a quiet place afterward to be with my disappointment. Feelings are like little children who can be hushed only so long before they throw a tantrum. Then, perhaps in minutes, instead of hours, or at least hours, instead of days, I will be able to find pleasure in what I've done. I will first grieve my Fs, and then I will celebrate my As.

—*Samantha Ducloux*

A Lesson Learned

She taught junior and senior high school English and also had senior homeroom.

She was a tall woman, taller than most of her students and most of the men faculty. She wore tennis shoes in school, unheard of for women of that time, and walked very erect. Her snow-white hair never appeared to be combed. She wore no makeup and no jewelry, except for a wristwatch. Her eyesight was poor, so she wore Coke-bottle-thick eyeglasses all the time and still bent closely over the work on her desk. She had the habit of jutting out the tip of her tongue when she was concentrating or when she was perturbed. It seemed she wore the same long white dress, which came down to the top of her tennis shoes, all the time.

Her initials were A. W. A. The W was for Wadsworth, she told us one time. We knew very little about her—nothing about her family, where she came from, or her background—only that she had graduated from Smith College. She lived alone in a big house close to the school. She walked to school as the weather allowed, and she was at her homeroom desk as soon as the janitor opened the building in the morning.

It seemed to us she had been teaching at the high school forever. My brother, who was five years older than me, had her for English and homeroom. He had advised me to make sure to do my homework, to be prepared in class, and never to lie to her. He said she was a hard marker, but that she was fair.

Her classes were lively, and she made sure that everyone became involved in class in some way. Her classes were interesting, informative, and, surprisingly, a lot of fun. We learned without even realizing she was teaching.

She loved poetry, so we conjectured that the Wadsworth middle name indicated some mysterious family background having to do with poetry, but we never found out. Poetry was an important part of her class work. Much time in class was given over to reading and trying to understand what the poets had written.

She also made a point and an effort to know her pupils. She knew the level at which each of us could work and learn, and she gave special attention to those of us needing it. I don't recall ever telling her I had played varsity basketball and baseball or that I had been junior class president and *pro merito*, but she knew. She said she liked my book reports and my written work, and she said my work represented honesty, integrity, and industry.

In those days, the Sunday *New York Times* published a complete separate section called *Aviation*. Somehow she knew of my interest in flying, so every Monday morning that section appeared on my homeroom desk, neatly rolled up and secured with a rubber band.

Early in the year, she asked me whether I planned to take the annual senior class trip to Washington. I told her it didn't seem possible, given my family's financial situation. She told me she needed somebody to take care of her rock garden and to do some other chores around her home. The job would pay two dollars for every Saturday I worked. Thanks to her help, I did make the class trip. I later learned that she had made work arrangements for other people in our class to help them make the trip, too.

Nobody in her classes could ever be considered a teacher's pet. She would allow us to get only so close to her before she would put up a barrier. But I had the feeling I came as close to being her favorite as any student ever had.

Her senior class final exam reflected her love for poetry, one poem in particular. She had never before required us to recite any poems from memory in class. However, for the final exam, she expected every pupil to recite from memory the last verse of "Thanatopsis." The recitation was to be fifty percent of the exam grade, just as it had been every year before.

She explained that because we were graduating to real life, this verse perfectly described how we should live our lives. She said that in the last verse of his poem, William Cullen Bryant had stated clearly and eloquently a simple philosophy for life that was a complete lesson in itself.

The method for our recitation finals was simple. She was at her homeroom desk very early in the morning every day. During the rest of the day, when she was not in class, she worked at a small desk on the landing between floors. At either desk, she always sat with her head down, never looking up, completely focused on her work. She knew every pupil's voice on cue, so when someone sat down to recite the verse, she would simply make a mental note and later check off that pupil's name as having completed the oral part of the exam.

On the final deadline day, I had not learned the verse and there was no valid reason why I hadn't. In desperation, I hit upon what I thought was an easy way out. As I knew she never looked up when a pupil recited, all I had to do was sit down with the textbook in my lap opened to the poem and carefully read it.

I didn't know then nor do I know now whether she accidentally kicked my foot or whether she knew exactly what she was doing. As she kicked my foot, the heavy English textbook landed on the floor with a bomblike explosion.

She looked up quickly, and the expression on her face was something I have never forgotten. She said, "James, you have failed."

I quickly picked up the book and walked away. That night, I memorized the last verse of "Thanatopsis." The next morning I stood in front of her desk in homeroom and asked her if I could say something. She didn't look up or answer. I recited the verse:

> So live, that when thy summons comes to join
> The innumerable caravan which moves
> To that mysterious realm, where each shall take
> His chamber in the silent halls of death,
> Thou go not, like the quarry-slave at night,
> Scourged to his dungeon, but, sustained and
>   soothed
> By an unfaltering trust, approach thy grave
> Like one who wraps the drapery of his couch
> About him, and lies down to pleasant dreams.*

Still, she did not look up or speak. I said "Thank you," and walked away. She gave me a failing grade for the exam, but I did graduate.

I did not speak with her again for nearly six years. Though I had continued with my life, that episode remained with me.

On a cold February day while I was home on leave from the Air Force after graduating from flying school, I decided to see her again. Without calling first, I drove to her home and rang the doorbell. She didn't seem to be surprised to see me; in fact, it seemed as though she had been expecting me. She hadn't changed one bit from the last time I'd seen her.

We had tea, and looking at my wings, she said she had expected I would do something about flying. We exchanged information about some of my classmates, and she surprised me with how much she knew about so many of them. Neither of us mentioned the episode that had bothered me for so long, and I wondered whether she remembered it. Somehow, I knew she did. When we said our good-byes, we both knew we would not meet again.

She continued teaching for many more years, and the last verse of "Thanatopsis" remained as fifty percent of her senior English final exam. She died at the age of 102.

I still have the two-ring notebook that my brother used in her classes and passed on to me. I used it in my classes with her and still have many of the book reports and other papers I wrote in her classes.

I have never forgotten that tall, white-haired teacher, nor have I forgotten the look on her face when she said I had failed. When she kicked my foot she taught me a lesson I'll never forget. To this day, my mantra is the last verse of "Thanatopsis." I recite it at least once a day, every day.

—James Eisenstock

*From "Thanatopsis," 1821, William Cullen Bryant.

Lost and Found

"I don't want to know who took the Alpha Smart. My only concern is that it is returned. If you know who took it, please try to convince them to bring it back. Two hundred dollars is a lot of Christmas presents." I looked at my class in frustration. The usual cacophony of voices and laughter was absent from the room, leaving only a wary silence.

Only weeks before I had extended myself by taking responsibility for the Alpha Smart cart, thirty tabletop word processors that aided my students with composition. Everyone seemed to love them. I had rearranged my classroom and my schedule to accommodate the little machines because I wanted the students to enjoy the writing process. Most of the other teachers in my department were becoming jaded. According to them, most teenagers didn't care about anything, especially schoolwork, so why go to the hassle of bringing in extra frills to spice up the curriculum? I was beginning to believe them. However, I cared about my students' success and I believed the tiny machines would help the weaker students to write more effectively.

It was a week before Christmas, and things at home were already tight. My husband had recently recovered from a back injury that had kept him out of work for two years. Now, he was just starting up a construction company, and money was trickling in very slowly. The two hundred dollars it would cost me to replace the Alpha Smart would destroy my plans to buy Christmas gifts for my family. I was already wondering how overdue I could be with my car payment before I'd be walking to work.

The days before the holiday break slowly ticked by. I tried to forget about the Alpha Smart and focus on the season. But I couldn't help feeling bitter about the loss and cynical about the kids, and wondering why I had entered a profession caring for other people's children. I could make a lot more money working in another field and get a great deal more appreciation. It was as if I had been slapped in the face. Even the teachers in the lounge seemed to be giving me a look that said, "I told you so," when the news got out that a thief was on the loose.

As I was dozing off before bed one night, my

evening prayers turned into a complaint. "Why does this have to happen right now?" I whined.

The next day at school was the last day before Christmas break. It was apparent that the Alpha Smart was history. I decided that the cart would have to go back to the learning lab. I would wash my hands of the hassle once and for all.

I was tidying up the cart for delivery when one of my students, Tara, came in.

"Hi, Mrs. Kilby. I have something for you," she said, handing me a gift bag.

I mustered a smile and did feel grateful. At least one of my students was thinking about me this holiday season.

"You're a sweetie," I said. "My husband and I aren't exchanging gifts this year, so I'll put it under my tree. That way I'll have more presents." I grinned.

"No," she said. "Promise me you'll open it today. You *have* to." Then she hurried out the door to her next class.

"Okay," I called after her.

I reached in and pulled out a note:

> Dear Mrs. Kilby,
> Hey, I just wanted to wish you a Merry Christmas and a Happy New Year. I belong to a club that helps people, and we pulled some money together to help you out. Please don't consider this

*a gift from me or from my club; consider it as God's
way of taking care of your needs.*

Love, Tara

I looked up at the empty doorway Tara had just
exited and then down at the gift bag with the illustration of a haloed angel on the front. I reached in
and pulled out a Ziploc bag filled with coins and
wads of bills. My eyes blurred as I counted. There
was almost two hundred dollars.

I found out later that my students had spear-
headed a collection to replace the Alpha Smart. The
money was a joint effort between the students in all
of my classes and Tara's club. It was a fabulous gift.
However, the money couldn't compare with the
other gift my students gave me: my belief in them. It
was as if they were God's little messengers, saving me
from the cynicism that was threatening to overtake
my heart, restoring my faith in the teenagers of today
and in my profession.

—*Erin K. Kilby*

Testing My Mettle

This can't be happening, I thought, as Mr. R., so large he had to duck his head to enter the classroom, headed straight for my desk, his anger evident by his body language and the snarling expression on his face. Everything seemed to move in slow motion, as everyone in the room held their breath. I wondered what would happen if I just bolted out of the room. *How could a simple joke with a student in my sixth-period class have led to this nightmare—an enraged parent storming into my classroom ready to do . . . what?* I didn't want to know.

The sixth-period class was a talented group of kids who were motivated and mature enough that I could joke around with them and still maintain order and accomplish much during class time. A playful but productive environment was standard operating procedure, and both the students and I worked hard but kept it light and had fun. Mary R. was one of the brightest and most genial students in the class.

Mary usually got straight As, so when she received a B– on a minor assignment, she came to see me before class. Mildly upset, she approached my desk to inquire about her grade. After a quick examination, I remarked that her answer to question number two was incorrect. Mary said in a loud voice that her father had given her that answer and he was not usually wrong. I read the answer again and emphatically stated the answer was wrong.

Mary came into class the next day and announced to the group that her father had reiterated the correctness of his answer and was furious with me. Thus began a daily tease routine that lasted at least a month. Every day in class Mary would tease about how angry her dad was getting and that he expected me to both rectify my error and apologize.

In the spirit of good fun and to comply with my role in Mary's charade, I would put up my dukes and exclaim, "Tell your dad to meet me after school in the back parking lot: Marquis of Queensberry Rules apply. And no hitting south of the equator."

Mary would playfully warn, "My dad is tough, and he is angry."

To which I'd reply, "I've taught driver's education for ten years—nothing scares me."

This banter lasted about four weeks and then was forgotten.

Open school night was a ritual I enjoyed. It was always fun to guess which students' parents were present. As the evening progressed, I worked through my schedule and the sixth-period parents finally came in for their twenty-minute slot. Unbeknownst to me, Mary's dad, Mr. R., had not entered the room with the other parents. I also had no idea that he was six feet, ten inches tall and weighed about 350 pounds.

About three minutes into my presentation, the door flew open with tremendous force, pushed aside with the largest human hand I'd ever seen. The giant attached to that hand burst into the room, saying, "I am Mary's dad and I am here to have it out with you." As his huge form advanced toward me, he said, "That's right: you and me, one-on-one."

Fear penetrated every pore of my body. I looked at the parents sitting near the front of the room, straining to get farther back in their seats. They were clearly not about to jump into the impending massacre. I sat at my desk, immobile and speechless.

Then, Mr. R. was standing right next to my chair, so close I could see the creases on his huge hands, and suddenly . . . he bent forward, kissed me on the cheek, and thanked me for making his daughter love history. The parents applauded, and Mr. R., smiling broadly, went and sat at one of the students' desks.

I have often wondered whether the parents' applause was in appreciation of my teaching abilities, Mr. R.'s excellent acting job, or relief in not being witness to a parent-teacher pummeling.

—*Glenn Hameroff*

The Creative One

"Don't call me stupid!" Katie yelled, tears welling in her eyes. She glared at the kids riding away on their bicycles, then turned and ran into the house.

I stood there, stuck, trying to think of what I could do to make Katie feel better and, to be honest, feeling more than a little guilty. Katie was my little sister and I was usually very protective of her, to the point that people often referred to me as her second mom. But I suddenly realized that I had been the mean sister and called her stupid sometimes, too. I just hadn't realized until that moment how much being called stupid hurt Katie.

It was a Saturday, and Katie had just met with her first-grade teacher for some extra help with reading. After the lesson, Katie and her teacher had gone to Dairy Queen for a chocolate-dipped ice cream cone, where they were spotted by the boys on the bikes. They had guessed, correctly, that she was being tutored and later taunted her when they rode by the house. After that, Katie refused any special tutoring or help.

I'm not sure how it came to be that Jenny, our oldest sister, and I loved reading so much and that Katie viewed books with plain hatred. When we tried to read together, the words didn't seem to make sense to her. Sometimes she would get so frustrated she would slam the book shut. Yet, there was no denying she had a quick mind. Anyone playing "Memory" with her could see that. There was no beating Katie at that game.

Jenny and I always looked forward to Christmas and the huge cache of books we would eagerly unwrap each year: Nancy Drew. Trixie Belden. Agatha Christie. Books on horses for Jenny. Books on travel adventures and whodunits for me. For a few years my parents tried to give Katie books, too. Katie threw tantrums at such efforts, and my parents eventually started giving Katie paint sets and modeling clay instead. Though Katie loved art, she would look at her gifts, steal glances at ours, and sigh as if she felt like a failure.

As years went by, Katie became increasingly resentful of her teachers' and our parents' efforts to stimulate her interest in books and reading. She would cry and get jittery or hyper when she had to read for school or for the summer book clubs at the neighborhood library.

"Stop trying to shove books down my throat," she would cry.

When our mother started introducing Jenny and me as the "honor-roll twins" and Katie as the "creative one" in the family, that was it. Game over. She wasn't going to play. There just didn't seem to be any way she could measure up to her sisters. Heels dug in, Katie made a declaration: She would learn what she needed to know only in class or on television. She was *not* going to read *any* books for *any* reason *ever*.

Increasingly, art became a haven for Katie. In art class, there were no books to read, and her teachers seemed to believe in her abilities. Jenny and I didn't take art classes, so she didn't feel in competition with us. There were no bad grades or nagging feelings of failure. There was no such thing as "stupid" art. In high school she won an award for a chalk drawing she did of a flamingo, and my parents proudly framed several of her pictures for their walls. She blossomed and found happiness in her art—that is, until she and her friends started thinking about colleges and took the required college entrance exams.

I'll never forget the look on Katie's face the day her college test scores came in the mail. I walked into the family room to find her sitting in our dad's big chair with her chin buried in her chest, her sandy blond hair hiding her face. She raised her head and looked at me with utter despair.

"I don't think I can go to college," she said in a flat voice.

In our household, this was a profound announce-ment. There were two things that a Jackson daughter knew and accepted as gospel from earliest memory. First, Dad's word was final, and second, you were going to college. Amen.

Katie's test scores were very low, as were her aca-demic grades in high school. But until that moment, I don't think Katie ever seriously considered that she might not get accepted to a college. Once again, my little sister's eyes welled with tears. She wiped them away, got up, walked slowly and dejectedly up the stairs to her room, and quietly shut the door.

Now, despite my father's authoritarianism, or perhaps because of it, there lurks within us Jackson girls a rebellious streak. It didn't take long for it to spark in Katie. She was going to apply to college, anyway. Though she didn't have quite enough courage to apply to her dream school, Michigan State University, she applied to another school where she thought she might have a better chance to get in. And she was accepted, with provisions.

Katie was required to take some remedial courses to get up to speed. Her initial reaction was to resent the special requirements and to focus on the "low achiever" title that seemed to be tattooed on her forehead. But then Katie made a decision: She would stop blaming everyone else for her hatred of reading—and she would learn to read.

Katie took in-depth notes in her college classes and then carefully rewrote them several times, incorporating what she was able to comprehend in her reading. For the first time, she began to participate, timidly, in class discussions and to ask her professors about topics that confused her. Slowly, her confidence built and she began to feel like part of the class. With her growing insights and abilities, she also saw herself as an important contributor to class discussions and to the classroom learning experience as well.

Then came the blow.

The results of the tests she took at the end of her freshman year that would enable her to pass out of the remedial track were in.

"Ms. Jackson, you have a tenth-grade reading level," the test administrator told her. "It is highly doubtful that you will be able to complete college."

Katie was stunned: *a sophomore in college reading at the level of a sophomore in high school?* The low reading scores, coupled with the administrator's blunt assessment that she had little chance of making it through college, crushed and crippled Katie.

Katie had panicked just before taking the tests.

She'd never done well on tests, and she knew she was still behind with her reading. But Katie had calmed herself by focusing on her recent, freshman-year successes. She never expected to score so poorly or to be told so frankly that she was likely to fail at her goal of obtaining a college degree.

Katie's first response was utter despair. She had several emotional breakdowns and called herself worthless, no good, and, yes, stupid. But her resilient, rebellious Jackson spirit kicked in, and Katie started to get angry. Then she got very angry. She got so mad that she swore to prove the insensitive test administrator wrong, even though doing so meant risking big-time failure. So began one of the toughest battles of Katie's young adult life.

Katie enlisted help. She accepted the emotional support of friends and family, and for the first time, she let our mother read her papers and help her learn to write. Katie stopped comparing herself with her college roommates and friends, and she began to study three or four hours more a day than any of them, often while they were out having fun. Month after month, year by year, Katie caught up. She learned that she was smarter than she'd thought and just had to work a little harder. Then, she reached an electric milestone: her first four-point semester grade average. I was happy to share with her that I, one of the "honor-roll twins," had never gotten a four-point semester in college.

I am so proud of Katie for her college achievements, but I am even more proud of what she has done with them. Katie became a teacher. She worked hard to succeed not only for her own benefit, but also to prevent other kids from being left behind as she had been.

Knowing what it is like to feel insecure and to struggle academically, Katie wanted to learn how to provide a positive learning environment and to give kids a feeling of success and to ensure they learned to read early in their schooling. Katie dedicated herself to finding a variety of alternative teaching methods to reach the students who, like her, are unable to learn using conventional methods. Her sensitive and determined nature helps her draw out those students who are withdrawn or resistant. Her creativity and artistic talents have served her well in both connecting with and teaching her students.

Today, Katie teaches third grade in the same school where she didn't learn to read. With each passing year, more students vie to have their children placed in Katie's class. She beams with justifiable pride when any of the school's staff refers to her as the creative one.

Last year, Katie became the first person in our family to earn a master's degree. She completed a wonderful graduate program that emphasizes creativity in teaching—from Michigan State University.

Her next goal is to write children's books that help children learn to read. No one would think to call Katie stupid now.

Katie has made no little impact on her big sister. Her courage and dedication continually inspire me. In fact, I recently left the *Fortune* 500 world behind me. I've switched careers. This fall, I started my first job as a teacher. I just hope I can measure up to my sister Katie.

—*Abby Warmuth*

What This Teacher Understands

What this teacher understands is that our son's learning disabilities and attention deficit hyperactivity disorder (ADHD) are legitimate disabilities.

What this teacher understands is that our son takes an amphetamine medication, a form of "speed." This medication helps him to focus on what's being taught in class and also diminishes some of the excess energy created by ADHD.

What this teacher understands is that when our son is on this medication, he doesn't eat, feels dazed, is nauseous, has constant headaches, and the neck tic caused by use of this medication gets worse.

What this teacher understands is that without this amphetamine medication, our son will have a harder time controlling his moods (like a bike racing downhill with no brakes) and keeping quiet.

What this teacher understands is the strength and courage our son must have in order to endure the sometimes horrible side effects of the medication he takes and of the various medication combinations he's tried, so that he can be more compliant in school.

What this teacher understands is that there will be times when we, as parents, will grant our son the opportunity to come to school unmedicated so that he can feel less sedated.

What this teacher understands is the tremendous amount of frustration our son deals with every day because of his learning disabilities, as he struggles to keep pace with his classmates, to comprehend the material he is presented, and to communicate his thoughts on paper.

What this teacher understands is the bravery our son shows and the hurt he shoulders as he walks the halls of his middle school, ignoring the taunts of peers who refer to him as a "sped" (special education student).

What this teacher understands is that we, as parents, readily acknowledge and own our son's imperfections, do not condone his inappropriate behavior, and work hard to teach him the importance of taking responsibility for his actions.

What this teacher understands is the level of resilience our son must possess each day in order to go to school and be told that something wasn't done; or that something wasn't done correctly; or that something was answered correctly but because he wrote in green pen rather than pencil, his grade has been dropped from 100 to 80—and yet feel good about himself when he gets on the bus most mornings.

What this teacher understands is that if our son remembers his assignments two days more than he did the week before, it's progress, an *effort*. And that when he asks for help, he is acknowledging that he doesn't understand, which also means he is listening more and making more of an *effort* to understand.

What this teacher understands is that in taking our son to a tutor outside of school, we are not questioning his teachers' abilities; we are merely trying to augment what he is learning in school, so that he can catch up with his peers.

What this teacher understands is that with all the negative feedback our son hears throughout the day—"Why didn't you do this?" or "Why didn't you follow the instructions?" or "Why didn't you pay attention?"—we spend our time with him after school and on weekends focusing on the good things he has done (and can do), so he will stay motivated in trying to see beyond his limitations.

What this teacher understands is the gratitude our son and we, his parents, feel when she sends us e-mails acknowledging when our son has done something well or accomplished something good.

Because of this teacher's understanding—and because of her kindness, extraordinary efforts, acceptance of his imperfections, and sincere belief in our son—he has finally started to believe in himself. We have been so fortunate to have her in our lives.

—*Carol L. F. Kampf*

"What This Teacher Understands" was first published under the title "What My Son's Teacher Understands" in the June 2003 issue of *Attention Magazine*.

There's No Substitute

Where are all the substitute teachers? The subbing shortage is so severe in some cities that off-duty police and firefighters are sometimes hired to do the job. Now, this makes sense to me. When I get the call at 6:00 A.M., I bolt out of bed like it is a five-alarm fire.

The dispatcher on the phone says, "Middle school. Science. Report at seven o'clock, today."

"No problem," I say, dropping the phone and reaching for the navy blue suit I carefully laid out the night before. I lose a few minutes wrestling support pantyhose over my knees, but hope to save a few by applying makeup in the car's rear-view mirror and brushing my teeth in the school's water fountain.

Then it hits me: I'm not a science teacher. I teach English.

Of course, that excuse didn't work last week when

the school called and asked me to sub woodworking.

"Sorry," I told the dispatcher, picturing a class-room full of thirteen-year-olds wearing hockey masks and wielding power saws. "I'm an English teacher."

"Are you breathing?" she asked.

"Yes."

"Have a pulse?"

"Yes, but . . ."

"You'll do."

At the hectic breakfast table, my husband and two children ask which school I'm assigned to.

"Middle school," I tell them, trying not to notice the color draining from their faces. I reach for my briefcase, which contains a substitute teaching manual titled, *Everything You Always Wanted to Know about Subbing But Were Afraid to Ask*, with helpful hints like, "do not smile; students will think you're a pushover or suffering from a brain injury."

My third grader gives me the thumbs-up. "Hang tough, Mom."

"Have your cell phone?" my husband asks.

The kindergartner hugs me around the waist, depositing soggy Cheerios all over the suit.

"I'll see you this afternoon," I reassure them, as I try to extract myself from my daughter's embrace.

"Don't go, Mommy!" she wails as I race out the door. Even a kindergartner knows what I'm in for.

At the school, I follow the arrows to the office,

where I receive the red substitute folder that contains a map, rules, and six aspirin. If my deer-caught-
in-the-headlights expression leaves any uncertainty
as to why I'm there, the red folder I carry dispels all
doubt. Personally, I prefer the more direct method:
perhaps a scarlet letter *S* or a sign taped to my back
that reads "Kick Me. I'm the Sub."

In the classroom, I'm relieved to find detailed
instructions on the teacher's desk. Five classes of
eighth graders will be studying human reproduction.
I locate the textbook and homework assignments
and have begun to write my name on the chalkboard
when it hits me. *Human reproduction? Why not something simple, like flowers or mold spores?*

Suddenly feeling a little light-headed, I sit down
and hang my head between my knees. I fear that the
support hose has cut off circulation to my brain. I
fumble for the red folder, toss it on the floor, and position my face over it as I search for an important emer-
gency procedure: how to obtain a sub for the sub.

Taking deep breaths, I tell myself it could be
worse, like astrophysics or archery. After all, the
topic of reproduction isn't totally unfamiliar. I am the
first of eight successful reproductions on my parents'
part. I've even managed, with a little help from my
husband, to reproduce twice, not to mention my
expertise in caring for pet gerbils that reproduce on a
monthly basis. Peeking up from underneath the desk

as the students file in, I'm encouraged by the thought that I've come from a long line of accomplished human reproduction and am up for the lesson at hand. In addition to those qualifications, I'm breathing and have a pulse.

A boy with jeans sagging down around his kneecaps asks, "Feeling okay, lady?"

"Fine," I assure him, "just checking my notes."

I begin to suspect that this was a planned absence on their teacher's part. I picture Mr. Science Guy kicking back in some trendy little coffee shop, sipping cappuccino, listening to jazz, and congratulating himself on skipping the sex talk, while his sub is forced to stand in front of a classroom filled with hyperactive hormones and say words like "erection" and "gonads."

I begin by reading the assignment out loud—with expression. I put my heart into it, turning lesson plans into poetry. No one moves. They're quiet, listening. I finish and look up.

Silence.

Then it happens, I get a little too cocky, underestimate the precariousness of my situation, and I . . . smile.

Immediately, Baggy Pants raises his hand.

"Question?" I ask, pointing to him, feeling confident and in control.

Grinning, he leans back in his chair and casually tosses his comment out like a pro: "There's nothing this class can teach me that I haven't already seen on cable or done with Jenny."

Another beat of silence, punctuated by a girl's scream (Jenny?), and then all hell breaks loose. I have to admire Baggy Pants's timing, honesty, and the expedient manner in which he slam-dunks the entire class. Deflated, I try in vain to interest them in completing the lesson, but they know the score and claim the prize—all forty-five minutes of it.

When the dismissal bell finally rings, I look up from my rereading of *Everything You Always Wanted to Know About Subbing*. Baggy Pants is the last one to file out the door.

He pauses and says, "Don't feel bad, lady, I don't respect any authority."

"Thanks." I know a compliment when I hear one.

As police and firefighters fill in for regular substitute teachers, I'll be the first to wish them well and pass on a little reading material. But I'm afraid that even sidearms and riot gear won't impress all the Baggy Pantses of the educational system.

As for me, I know I can count on one thing: The phone will ring again tomorrow morning.

"High school. Astrophysics. Report at seven ay-em."

"Astrophysics? No problem!"

—*Dawn FitzGerald*

They Wanted to Teach

Nathan and Robert were students of mine. For two years, I was their middle school science teacher and coach, and got to know them as well as any teacher can. Nathan and Robert knew each other but came from vastly different backgrounds.

Nathan grew up in a wonderful home. Both parents were stable, college educated, and attentive, and he had a lovely twin sister.

Nathan had everything going for him. He was handsome, intelligent, and well liked by everyone around him. On the athletic fields he learned leadership, and Nathan went on to become the high school's varsity quarterback. Scholastically, he always ranked near the top of his class without having to stretch himself. Nathan was a devout Christian, active in church and youth fellowship programs. I believe everyone saw the bright future awaiting Nathan. The world extends a welcome mat for kids like Nathan.

Robert grew up in a dysfunctional home. His mother was a drug addict and dealer. He never saw his father, didn't even know who he was.

Robert had nothing going for him. He was always in trouble, and by the time I met him, he'd been through every aspect of our social services system. A judge from the city where Robert had lived prior to his most recent offense sentenced him to a rural group home within our school district.

As a teacher, I dreaded the kids from the group home attending school alongside our innocent and naive rural students. The delinquents were likely to share their criminal skills with our vulnerable youth, and fights were inevitable between the displaced kids and the toughest of the farm kids. Most of the city kids failed every class and often ended up being expelled within weeks. Prior experience had dashed any hope of success I once held for these wayward students.

I met Nathan under the best conditions. I had been hired the previous year as a rookie teacher by his father, our new principal. Nathan's dad and I became good friends, and we talked about every-thing—including Nathan's scary habit of sleep-walking. I learned he even walked outside, through snow, without waking. We laughed about it then, but lacking any knowledge of how to solve the problem, we expressed our hope that he would outgrow it.

Nathan did grow up, though not as big physically as he would have liked. But spiritually and morally, he grew into one of the finest young adults I've ever known.

I met Robert under the worst conditions. The group home had a habit of bringing their newest charges straight from the courthouse to the schoolhouse, and I looked up one day to see the school secretary standing at my door. A greasy-haired Robert stood alongside her with his arms crossed over his chest. The class was in the middle of a test, so I quietly showed Robert to a seat and set him up with a textbook and a short reading assignment.

The student sitting directly in front of Robert had a question about the test. While I was bent over to talk privately with the other student, I felt something touch me on the back. Just as I began to explain the test question, I was kicked full force in the behind. I wheeled around to see Robert wearing an ear-to-ear smile as he glanced around the room seeking peer approval. He gleefully pointed out to everyone the "Kick Me" sign he'd stuck on my back moments earlier.

The other students sat in stunned silence waiting my response. They expected me to blow up. I didn't. I shared with everyone a philosophy I practice: If I take the time to get in their face and issue a lecture,

I do so because I feel the student is worth my time and energy. On the other hand, if you're expecting to get yelled at and don't, be very worried, because I've decided you're unworthy. I reserve my efforts for those I expect better from. No student had ever earned my seal of disapproval as quickly as Robert had. With that, I made my first impression on Robert, just as Robert had made his first impression on me—and I issued him a five-day suspension.

Nathan, on the other hand, had two great years in my classroom. A kind and honest student who genuinely cared about his education, his classmates, and his teachers, he consistently earned As and always received the attention of the cutest girls. I knew Nathan would succeed regardless of what I did as his teacher. School was too easy for him, but he never complained. His parents had raised him well, and he was a child anyone would be happy to claim as his or her own. Every year, I meet a few more kids like Nathan.

Robert struggled through his first year at my school. I'm sure he had been to many others, given that he'd bounced back and forth between his mom and different foster homes most of his life. I'm sure he thought that after a few months, the judge would let him go home. They always did. Six months or a year later, some anonymous judge would decide these kids had been magically healed and would return the ill-prepared adolescents to the same environment in which they'd failed to thrive before. I don't remember why that didn't happen this time for Robert, and he was with us for a while.

During his second year, Robert was drawn to the athletic fields, and to participate in sports, he had to pass his classes. Once he applied himself, we discovered that there was a bright young man lurking behind the tough ne'er-do-well front he had presented earlier. From that point forward, Robert earned As and Bs—and my respect.

Robert taught me a lot about second chances and about never giving up on any kid. He proved himself to be quite worthy of my time and energy—and so, I came to realize, is every "lost cause" who enters my classroom.

The summer after both Robert and Nathan graduated from middle school, I invited them and some of their friends for a day of waterskiing. For the last run of the day, Nathan drove the boat while Robert and I hopped onto inner tubes being pulled behind. I waited for the right moment and then jumped from my tube onto Robert's back. Shocked, he grasped onto the tube tightly. I whispered in his ear, "I haven't forgotten your first day of school. I don't get mad. I get even!" Then I wrapped my arms around him and tugged until I pulled him from the tube and into the water. We both came up for air laughing about the wrestling match we'd just had and about the incident that had brought us together two years earlier.

Not long after, a judge ruled that it was time for Robert to go home. Robert balked. He didn't want to return to a situation where he was likely to regress, where he lacked the support to continue his sports activities and academic achievements. He'd worked hard to pull himself out of a huge rut, and he wasn't willing to throw his chance of success away. He sued for emancipation from his mother and won. Counselors found a local family willing to be Robert's foster parents. The foster family and Robert grew together, and he continued on his path toward becoming a fine adult.

With new students every year needing my attention, I lost touch with Nathan and Robert. As with all my past students, I watched them complete high school from a distance. After graduation, Nathan announced his plans to attend college and become a teacher. No one was surprised—Nathan had been groomed throughout his life to teach and coach. However, when I heard that Robert, too, had elected to become a teacher, I was pleasantly surprised and very proud of his choice. *What a fine pair of teachers those two will make,* I thought. Both would bring fresh energy and compassion to an occupation where they could truly make a difference.

They never got that chance. Nathan and Robert

both died before they could finish college. Nathan fell from a third-story fraternity room while sleepwalking. Oh, how I wish I'd done more years earlier when his father had asked me for advice—maybe researched the causes and treatments for chronic sleepwalkers, or encouraged him to pursue medical help for Nathan. As horrible as I feel about doing nothing, I didn't know then what I know now—that sleepwalking can be dangerous—and I know I can't go back and change anything.

Robert died in a single-car accident while driving home to see his girlfriend. She lived in our school district, several hours from his college campus. It is believed he fell asleep at the wheel.

Each year at our school we give an award in Nathan's honor to the eighth-grade student who best exemplifies Nathan's positive characteristics. These students are acknowledged for their scholarship, character, citizenship, and school spirit. I serve on the committee that selects the winner, and each year it goes to a kid just like Nathan. There are always lots of great kids from good families to choose from.

As for Robert, last I knew his grave was still without a marker. His mother refused to buy or accept donations for one. No award is given in his memory. But each year I privately seek out the Roberts in my classes—the undiscovered gems hidden among dozens of emotionally needy students.

Most are out of sync with societal norms. They wear dark clothes. They listen to dark music. They see dark futures for themselves. With a few well-placed positive strokes, a few will suddenly shine like never before. There are too many of these kids, and their numbers seem to grow each year. During those delicate adolescent years, they straddle a precarious, imaginary fence separating right and wrong, good and bad. Lacking proper guidance, they make poor choices. If someone doesn't steady their balance until they're smart and secure enough to get off the fence, we lose them. I've lost more than I care to count.

Each year, the Nathans in my class make the job easier. The Roberts, though fewer in number, make my entire career worthwhile.

I cry every time I announce the name of the recipient for the Nathan award.

I smile every time I see a fence walker, like Robert, climb down on his or her own.

I'm glad that we have so many Nathan award nominees each year. It gives me hope.

I'm challenged by the increasing number of at-risk students I see before me each year.

I just wish Nathan and Robert were teaching in the rooms next to mine. We need them. I miss them.

—*Tony Phillips*

Grade School Lessons for a Lifetime

We crowded around the door, nudging to peer into the dark room, our eyes wide, looking for evidence of leprechaun sabotage.

Mr. Spataro had warned us the day before that leprechauns would come to cause mischief on the eve of St. Patrick's.

"Naw!" we'd said. "That's just another one of your stories."

"It's true," our teacher had said, the pain of insult apparent in his voice. "They will come."

And they had. Usually, Mr. Spataro waited for us in the bright, organized classroom. Today, he stood in the hall with us, insisting that the leprechauns had come, wreaking havoc in our absence and a general electrical outage in our classroom. We pushed at the backpacks in front of us until the first kids at the door finally tumbled in. We entered slowly, prepared to turn our backs and run if the little people were still there. Our desks lay on their sides, books spilled onto the floor. And the queerest green footprints, no bigger than a baby's, circled the room, even ran up the wall.

"Here!" Mr. Spataro shouted. He stood over the desk of Craig O'Connell, the most Irish of any of us. He grasped a small block of soap that sat on the desktop and held it up like Charlton Heston holding a stone tablet. It said "Irish Spring" on the wrapper. It was proof. The leprechauns had come. We were believers.

I was nine when we moved to Colorado. It was late September, and school had started a month earlier. I was the new girl with the funny accent and the glasses, ripe for teasing.

"I can't wait for you to meet Mr. Spataro. He's the best teacher we have." I followed the gray-haired principal and my mother down the institutional hallway. I didn't like the way Dr. Cussen described this new teacher. If a grown-up said a teacher was good, you knew you were in for the worst year of your life. I could just see this huge, black-toothed, hairy tyrant pacing in front of the blackboard, waving his hook, the poor students cowering behind their desks, their only hope of relief, a ticking clock.

The principal turned a corner. "Here we are." They stopped, and I ran into the back of my mother's skirt. Dr. Cussen knocked on the door. I had the sweats now. My heart swelled in my throat. I just knew he would be mean.

The door opened just a sliver. Out came a furry, whiskered face no bigger than a monkey's head. "Yes? What do you want?" The thing asked in a screeching voice.

Dr. Cussen looked at my mother and forced an apologetic giggle. "Mr. Spataro?" he started timidly, "I have a new student for you."

The puppet disappeared, and Mr. Spataro opened the door. He wasn't very tall. I could see right into his eyes; they had funny little creases around them, from too much laughing. His big black moustache twitched, and I could tell he was trying not to laugh right then.

"I'm so embarrassed. I hope you don't think it is like that around here all the time," Mr. Spataro said, his ears turning pink. He apologized to the principal, who looked nervously at my mother.

My mother had a confused smile on her face, but I could tell she thought he was okay. I did, too.

That year went too fast. My classmates and I ran to the classroom every morning, just to see what Mr. Spataro would do next. We wrote and illustrated our own books. We had lunchtime trips to Taco Time and challenge-the-teacher problem relays in math class. Then there were Mr. Spataro's stories. Usually his tall tales came tumbling out while he was reading a book to the class. He would stop in mid-sentence.

"Did I ever tell you about the time I was hiking and fell into some quicksand?" Dramatic pause. "I breathed through a bamboo stick for two days until I was rescued!" He shook the copy of *Tragedy of the Tar Pits* he had been reading, for emphasis (Charlton Heston again).

We didn't think to ask where he'd found a bamboo stick in the Rocky Mountains—or quicksand, for that matter. By the end of the year, we all believed that Mr. Spataro had a car that moved on land, sea, and air. We believed in leprechauns. We believed in the utility of bamboo sticks. And we believed in the magic of Mr. Spataro.

More than two decades later, I remember that year as if it were last. Mr. Spataro encouraged our enthusiasm for learning. He inspired us to explore the world around and within us, and to look outside the box. Among our ranks today we have a nurse, a musician, a real estate agent, a writer, business executives, computer wizards, moms, dads, and teachers. Mr. Spataro knew that we weren't just kids. He knew that we were impressionable, thinking and feeling young people who would grow up, for better or worse. And he knew that one teacher could make the difference, tipping the scales in favor of much better.

—*Julie Dunbar*

A Little Child Shall Lead Them

I had just opened my classroom door to the balmy spring afternoon when a woman entered and surveyed the bustling crowd of kindergarten children, my aide, and several volunteer mothers.

"Who's the teacher?" she asked.

I glanced around the room. Debbie was tying her classmate Leonard's shoelaces. "Now, watch so you can do it, too," she directed in her high-pitched voice.

"The teacher?" I said, smiling. "Oh, today it seems to be Debbie."

In the years I was surrounded by children in their first year of public school, they often amazed me with their innocent wisdom and unself-conscious interaction. I learned much from these "teachers"—five years old and three feet tall.

Of all my students, Jason, Bethanne, and Tahn stand out most in my memory. Tahn, a refugee from

Vietnam, joined my class one February. Like many children in that mostly Asian neighborhood, he started his school experience with little knowledge of English.

On the first day I handed out boxes of large Crayola crayons. Tahn splayed his out on his work space and tested each color on his sheet of newsprint. Then, with a grin of confidence, he picked up a crayon and drew a tree trunk. Within five minutes, he had drawn a tree, a strip of sky, and a smiling boy with black spiky hair.

When I looked down to admire his work, he picked up two blue crayons and gave me a quizzical look. He pointed to the purple crayon in another child's hand, then back to his box. No purple. I explained that we were sometimes sloppy about the crayons and they ended up in the wrong boxes. I spoke English at my normal speed and in my usual tone of voice, knowing that my words would make no sense to him.

Yet, he understood. He got up with a blue crayon and walked around the room inspecting boxes. When he found one without blue, he dropped it in, then extracted an extra red and searched for a box without red. He repeated this process with amazing efficiency. By the time others had finished their pictures, each box contained the correct eight colors. In a few minutes, Tahn had completed a task that usually took an aide a half hour.

Tahn breezed through all his activities quickly, then looked around the room to find something that needed organizing, cleaning up, or rearranging. With art projects, he finished first, always. He would go to a child who was having difficulty applying papier-mâché, getting two pieces of clay to stick together, or cutting along lines on a piece of paper. At first, I wondered if he would take the experience away from the other child, but I soon found that he acted like a coach, showing the other child how to do the task.

That spring, I collected plastic berry baskets and taught the class how to weave rug yarn through the holes. As usual, Tahn finished first and then helped others. Meanwhile, I picked up almost-finished baskets and tucked in the last bits of yarn. I continued this process while my aide took the children to recess. A little head emerged near my hands. Tahn watched while I repaired a particularly pathetic basket.

"Tahn, you didn't go outside with everybody else."

I did not know whether he actually understood my words or just the essence of their meaning, but he answered, "I watch."

I over turned the basket and maneuvered the last bit of yarn into place. I plopped it in front of Tahn. "There!"

He rewarded me a wide, impish grin and said, "Veddy gooot, Teacha!"

The year Bethanne showed up, I had been blessed with a small class. It enabled me to give individual time to each child, and no one needed it more than Bethanne.

Not that I could teach her much of a cognitive nature. She had no language skills—neither English nor her native Philippine Ilicano dialect. A seven-year-old weighing 130 pounds, she communicated with grunts, couldn't hold a pencil or a crayon, and pawed through books with little control of her hands. Her parents had been afraid to bring her to school.

But she could hug. She would throw her arms around me and look into my face, beaming. She embraced her much-smaller classmates, too, but always with gentleness.

We often sat on the floor in a circle, which was hard for Bethanne, but she managed to plop down, turn around, and with her hands on the floor, hoist herself back up again. When she was seated, children scrambled to sit next to her, leaning up against her comforting bulk while she sat passively, a faint smile on her face.

The other children tried to teach her to talk. I remember Jamilla sitting with her, an open book on

Bethanne's lap. "This is a sheep, Bethanne. Say 'sheep.'" Bethanne only smiled.

Once, while taking the class to the gym, we passed a group of older children. "Hey, look, there goes that big, fat kindergarten girl," someone yelled, and his classmates laughed.

The kindergartners did not. When we got back to the classroom, Douglas said, "Those big kids made fun of Bethanne." Others nodded solemnly.

The school counselor and nurse arranged testing by a medical team, and we were told what Bethanne's parents had been afraid to find out. Bethanne's mental capacity was so limited and her physical size so unmanageable that she probably would not live into adulthood. She would never be able to care for herself beyond the most basic functions.

I realized that I did not have the skills to give her what she needed—except for the loving environment that she experienced with the children in our wonderful little group. But she needed more. She was placed in a special education class at another school, and I hoped it was for the best. Several weeks later at a meeting, I met the aide from her new class.

"Are you the person who sent us that obese girl who wants to hug everybody all the time?" he asked me.

"You mean Bethanne?" I said. "That's how she communicates. She needs to love, and hugging is the only way she can express it."

"Well, let me tell you what that loving lump did." His sarcasm was acid. "She escaped the classroom a week or so ago, went into the parking lot, and snapped the antennas off all the faculty cars."

I tried to imagine her rage. *At her new class? At me, for abandoning her?* I felt sick.

I swallowed, forcing myself to control my anguish and anger. "What do you plan to do about her?" I asked.

He told me that the school was working on a placement at the experimental school on the University of Washington campus. A few weeks later, Bethanne was transferred to one of the best places for mentally disabled children in the country.

Another year, when I greeted my kindergartners at the classroom door after Christmas break, I noticed that many children were wearing new jackets, hats, mittens, and backpacks, obviously Christmas bounty. During our opening circle, we admired each other's newly acquired possessions: clothes, a pair of shoelaces, socks, a barrette, a haircut. I showed them my new watch. One pair of items stood out among the new treasures: Jason's sparkling silver sneakers. We observed the look of joy on Jason's brown face.

"Hightops," he told us proudly. "And purdy soles." He lifted one foot with his hand and pivoted his leg for all to see the pattern of colored lines and circles on the bottoms of the new shoes.

For recess, the children took out balls, jump ropes, and chalk. I watched them fan out in their habitual directions, each group finding its own area on the playground. Jason and the usual cluster of runners lined up at the edge of the schoolyard: taut, expectant, eager.

"Ready, set, go!" they yelled.

I watched them take off. Five boys and two girls sprinted away from the starting line, Gary in the lead. Gary, who always took off on the word "set," usually arrived first at the edge of the concrete and tumbled, panting, onto the grass before the others joined him, laughing, piled into a disorganized heap. Winning was important to Gary because his older brothers played hockey and he understood competition. The rest of the small runners, Jason included, were content just to feel the power of their bodies sprinting through space. I never intervened. Soon enough, in a year or two, they would learn about being the first, the best, the strongest, and playing by the rules.

But this was a special day for Jason. I watched him take off on "go," and his obvious excitement propelled him faster than usual. His new shoes gleamed like hubcaps in the sunlight, a blur of speed. He left the others far behind, caught up with Gary, and reached the grassy finish line well ahead of the veteran winner.

"Oh, man," I heard Gary complain. "It's those shoes, Jason. No fair!"

Jason ran up to me, chest heaving. I looked down at his excited face.

"You were great, Jason!" I said. "How did that feel?"

"It's my sneakers," he gasped. "They're really fast. I can go like the wind now! My Grandpa told me I'm gonna be an Olympic star, just like Jesse Owen!"

In the following days and weeks, I watched Jason live up to his belief about the shoes. He not only ran the races, he ran everywhere, and I enjoyed seeing his skill, speed, and agility improve daily.

That spring, a new student joined our class. From the moment he entered, the other children were agog with excitement. Tanned by the Hawaiian sun of his former home, fully a head taller than most of his new classmates, Samuel exuded confidence and maturity far beyond his years. At recess, each group vied for his participation, but he chose to join the runners.

"Ready, set, go," the sprinters yelled.

Gary left at "set," Jason at "go." Samuel hesitated, but only briefly, before catching on. He sped away and overtook the two in the lead. The new boy was beauty, grace, and speed in motion. His muscled, sun-browned body and gleaming honey-blond hair reminded me of the Greek messenger god, Mercury.

I watched as he ran far past the indefinite finish line and to the end of the playground.

Poor Jason, I thought, dismayed. He had slowed down and then actually stopped to watch Samuel. His mouth hung open, but only for a few seconds. As Samuel walked back toward the others, who now lay sprawled on the grass, I watched in amazement as Jason approached him and, extending his hand, pumped Samuel's hand vigorously.

Jason trotted back to me, his eyes shining with excitement. "Did you see that new boy, Samuel?" he asked.

"Yes, I did," I replied. "He's pretty good, isn't he?"

"He runs so fast," Jason panted. "He runs just like the wind! He's gonna be an Olympic star someday!"

I hunkered down and hugged Jason, my eyes welling up with tears, and I thought, *Someday, Jason, when I grow up, I want to be just like you.*

"Maybe so," I told him. "But I know you'll be a star, for sure. You have enthusiasm and a generous heart."

"Yeah." Jason grinned. "And silver sneakers."

For nine years, I nurtured my kindergarten students, rewarded cooperation and creative expression, and planted the academic skills needed to launch them into the first grade. But often the teaching flowed both ways. Many times, I felt more like student than teacher, learning from such role models as Tahn, the organizer and friendly coach, affectionate Bethanne's compassionate classmates, and Jason of the generous heart.

—*Annemarieke Tazelaar*

The Educated Dude

Of all my students in eleven years of teaching, Mac holds a special place in my memory. Mac was in my second period English class. He sat in the fourth seat of the third row behind a larger boy who completely hid him from my view. Mac was small for his age. I can picture him now in his standard outfit of faded blue jeans and a plaid shirt with several pencils in the pocket, his sandy brown hair uncombed, his blue eyes twinkling. He had plenty of friends and fit smoothly into the group.

Mac seemed to be attentive and to work during class, so I was surprised to discover after the first few weeks of school that he had not handed in even one assignment. And, even though he wasn't doing his assignments, he wasn't causing trouble, so he was the kind of kid I might easily have overlooked.

Something about Mac, however, drew my

attention and made me curious to know more about him. Perhaps it was his independent spirit, the nonchalant way he walked into the class each day, greeting his friends and bouncing into the seat behind his desk. Still, I did not act on my inclination until the guidance counselor asked me to complete a progress report on Mac.

"His parents have asked for a team meeting," she said. "They think Mac is learning disabled or emotionally disturbed or lazy. They aren't sure what, but they think there is something wrong with him. What can you tell me?"

I couldn't give the guidance counselor much information about Mac. "He's not all that interested in English. He doesn't turn his work in very often," I said.

"But," I hastened to add, "he's not disruptive and he seems like a happy kid. Quite cheerful, in fact. I could be wrong, but I don't see any signs that Mac has a serious problem. I like him."

When I checked in my grade book, I was surprised and embarrassed to find that I did not have a single grade recorded for him. Mac had not even turned in weekly spelling tests that the whole class did together. Somehow, he was slipping through the cracks. *From now on,* I thought, *I need to pay closer attention to Mac.*

The process of getting to know Mac began the next day. I was sitting at my desk grading the weekly spelling tests while the class worked on a vocabulary assignment. I noted that, once again, there was no paper from Mac in the stack. Out of the corner of my eye I watched Mac casually sauntering down the aisle so that he could toss a wadded-up piece of notebook paper into the trashcan.

"Having trouble, Mac?" I asked.

"Naw," he muttered cheerfully and ambled back to his seat, pausing for a word here and there with his classmates.

The following day I assigned the class a short essay in which the students were told to describe an activity they enjoyed. After they began working, I wandered down the rows of desks, encouraging the students, chatting with them about their ideas for the essay, making my way as unobtrusively as possible toward Mac. When I reached his desk, I saw his arm ease over to cover his paper so that I couldn't see what was on it, a behavior that I had grown accustomed to over the years.

"Any problems?" I asked.

"No." He smiled in his usual happy-go-lucky way.

"Make sure you finish something by the end of the period," I said.

"By the way, class," I announced, "I'm collecting whatever you are able to complete today."

"Why can't we finish it for homework?" one student asked.

"Today, I want to see what you've done in class. I'll hand your papers back tomorrow, and you can work on them some more, if you'd like."

A few students made the standard moans and groans, but no one appeared to be especially disturbed by my announcement, least of all Mac, who continued to hover over his paper until I had passed by and out of range. I continued my maneuvering around the classroom for a while and then went back to my desk and sat down, watching Mac as much as possible without being obvious.

Until then, I had not taken a close look at Mac's work habits. Now, I saw that he was inattentive to his assignment, spending most of his time chatting quietly with other students around him. I saw him ask a girl for a better pencil. Then he went up to the pencil sharpener, stopping now and then to check on what his friends were doing. Once back in his seat, he wrote for a few minutes and then gazed out the window.

"Well, I know he has written something," I thought to myself.

Near the end of the period I announced that it was time to turn in the day's work. "Okay, class, time is almost up. Finish the sentence you are working on and get ready to pass in your papers. Be sure to put your name on the paper," I added.

My announcement was the signal Mac was waiting for. He got up and walked toward the trashcan, wadding up his paper as he went. I moved quickly to stop his mission.

"Not today, Mac," I said, cutting him off. "I want you to turn in whatever you finished."

"It's no good," he said with his likable boyish grin still in place.

"I don't care," I told him. "I want to see what you've done so far."

Mac looked at me curiously, considered rebellion, and then decided to humor me. Reluctantly, he handed me his paper.

"Thanks," I said, smoothing out the wrinkles. "I'm looking forward to reading this." I spoke matter-of-factly and immediately turned away to speak to the class. "Please pass in your papers right now. The bell is going to ring any minute. Please don't leave without giving me your work," I emphasized for Mac's benefit, to ensure he didn't think I was singling him out for special attention.

The next hour was my planning period. I eagerly flipped through the papers to find Mac's crinkled one. He had written two or three short sentences about going hunting with his father in ordinary looking, legible handwriting. I could find no reason why he would throw it away rather than hand it in.

I smoothed out the paper and circled one misspelled word and wrote the correct spelling on the paper. I thought for a several minutes about the kind of comment to write. Finally I wrote, "Good start. Tell me more about hunting." After more deliberation, I wrote "C−" at the top of the paper. So that Mac would not be suspicious, I wrote a comment on all of the other students' essays as well.

The next day I passed out the papers at the beginning of the period and told the students to read my comments and to continue working on their essays. As soon as I had a chance, I walked near Mac's desk and struck up a conversation with the boy who sat next to him. Just as I hoped, Mac quickly became interested in what I was saying and I was able to draw him into the conversation. Casually, I mentioned that Mac had written about a topic that I found interesting—going hunting.

Mac gave me a quick, suspicious look and then decided that my comment was genuine. I left him and his classmate engaged in a conversation about Mac's topic. A few minutes later I cautioned both of them to get back to work.

"Let's get those ideas down on paper," I said encouragingly.

At the end of the period, Mac turned in the revised paper, which now had two more sentences. I was jubilant with this small success. I wrote "Much better!" in the margin, and gave it a grade of C+.

From then on, Mac became the focus of as much subtle, special attention as I could give him.

My moves were carefully planned, but my goal was simple. By the end of the year, Mac was going to have enough confidence in himself to hand in his assignments and he would begin to value his education.

After the evaluation and team meeting Mac's parents had requested, the guidance counselor stopped by to tell me that the staff had advised the parents to relax. Everyone concurred that Mac was normal but perhaps slightly immature. His parents were persuaded not to make any major decisions about their son, and the counselor promised to keep them informed of any changes in his behavior.

During the next few weeks I chatted with Mac whenever an opportunity presented itself. If he turned in his work, I commented favorably. If he did not turn in an assignment, I expressed disappointment. Slowly but surely, the papers started to come in regularly.

One day I suggested that he pay closer attention to spelling and punctuation. "Otherwise," I said, "your writing is quite good."

The flattery and added pressure were too much for Mac.

"Hey, Mrs. Walker." He looked me directly in the eye, unsmiling and speaking seriously for the first time since I'd known him. "I don't want to be no educated dude."

He had me there. Making him into an educated dude was my plan exactly. Perhaps I had no right to try to change Mac's self-image or to make him become someone he didn't want to be, even if it was, in my opinion, for his own good.

"Well, Mac," I responded after reflecting on his comment, "there may be some advantages to being an educated dude that you haven't considered."

I turned away and walked toward another student who was standing at my desk with a question. Out of the corner of my eye, I saw Mac give me a small, unwilling smile. He and I both knew that we were engaged in a struggle and that I was, at that point, winning.

The campaign to increase Mac's confidence in his academic ability continued day by day as I made occasional calculated comments to him. One day when I thought he was ready, I wrote "Excellent work!" on a particularly interesting composition he'd written and gave it a B, his first one. When I handed back the papers, I saw Mac show his to the student who sat next to him. He was pointing with pride at the grade. I knew then that I had won more than just a skirmish.

On his next report card, Mac got a C in English for the semester. The guidance counselor told me that he'd been doing better in his other classes, too. Mac himself confided to me that his parents were happy with his grades for the first time in his life.

"If I keep doing good, I'm supposed to get a dirt bike for my birthday."

As the year went by, Mac and I continued our quiet friendship. He wasn't the type to come by after school to see me or to give me a Christmas card. But once or twice when we passed in the hall, Mac acknowledged me by saying, "Hi!"

It was a lot from Mac, and it was enough for me.

—*Bonnie L. Walker*

An earlier version of this story was published under the title "Mac Wore a Mask of Indifference" in the March/April issue of *Learning 92.*

Champion of Children

She stood peering into the bathroom mirror, her finger tracing a wrinkle at the corner of her right eye. Time had become a nuisance to her. She wanted it to slow down. The gradual decline of her arthritic hands, however, seemed only to confirm that time would continue its forward advance. As she turned on the sink faucet and splashed cool water on her face, she began wondering about her life. *Had it been well spent?*

Reaching for a towel, she thought of the ordinary life she'd led, accomplishing nothing that made her stand out. It's not that she wanted fame and fortune or prestige and power. She just wanted to feel like she had made a difference in the world. At sixty-three years old, with nothing to show for a life among children but a tattered memory book hidden amidst junk in her attic, Mrs. Monroe felt less than accomplished. She felt empty.

Petroleum jelly has served my face well, she thought, as she dug into the ointment to moisturize her skin. People often remarked how much younger she looked than her years, a trait she attributed to Vaseline, which she'd used since childhood.

Elmer's snoring jolted her out of her musing. He was sleeping in today. It was 7:00 A.M., and after more than thirty-five years of teaching, her internal clock was still set to get up and go, so she would have to start her day without him. She went to the kitchen. Opening the window blinds, she wondered if Elmer had noticed her aging. He didn't seem to, but then Elmer noticed little. Like the time when Miss Lucille, their next-door neighbor, ran over their lawn and into the mailbox, crushing their begonias. *If Elmer didn't notice that, how could he notice that my youthfulness has slipped away*, she reasoned, almost with a smile.

Mrs. Monroe began preparing coffee she would have preferred to share with Elmer. The smell of French vanilla waltzed about her, teasing her. Disregarding its call, she smoothed down her soft, silvery hair and buttoned the top of her house robe, which seemed to dwarf her shrinking frame, and went outside to collect the newspaper. Her eyes scanned the neighborhood, reminding her of its unassuming appeal. Despite the detachment of folks that lived around her, it was where she wanted to live, particularly since she'd retired. Little went on there. It was Saturday, and the only thing hoppin' was the squirrels dashing across the streets and up the Cypress trees.

As she went back inside, she couldn't help thinking about times when the neighborhood residents were not so aloof and when her house was a clubhouse for the neighborhood children. Somehow, the kids ended up in her home after school, after church, and after mandated time spent with their families. And the parents never seemed to mind her mothering their children. "Oh, he's over at the Monroes," or "She's with the teacher," they would say. Now, she barely knew the kids in her neighborhood.

Settling at the kitchen table with her cup of coffee, she noticed it immediately: The silence of a house with no children. Hers had grown up and moved out. Her grandchildren were teens, too busy with music, fashion, and dating to want her and Elmer's company, especially on a Saturday. And the children she'd taught were now nothing more than mere memories—but at least she had the memories.

She most enjoyed remembering the first day of class. Before her students' arrival, she would painstakingly transform the classroom into a children's paradise with pictures in bright, bold colors and animated props. No matter how warm and welcoming she made the room, at least one of her kindergartners would cry to go home. Others would hang on to her coattails as if she had given birth to them herself. By the time the school year ended, they were as comfortable in her classroom as they were in their own backyards. If their ease in her class wasn't evident by June, it surely was by August when school began again. One or two of her former students would inevitably wander out of their first-grade class and back to her classroom, seeking out what was familiar and cherished.

The telephone's loud ringing startled her from her reverie.

"Hello," she answered.

"Mrs. Monroe?" It was an unrecognizable voice.

"Yes."

"Mrs. Monroe, the elementary school teacher?"

"Yes."

"It's me, Amy," the caller replied.

There have been lots of Amys, Mrs. Monroe thought and said nothing.

"Amy Binkingham. I mean Amy Wilson. You taught me at J. T. Butler Elementary. I was in your third-grade class."

"Oh, my goodness! Amy! Of course! Who could forget that fiery red hair . . . and all those freckles?" Mrs. Monroe fairly bellowed in delight. "How are you, sweetheart?"

"I'm fine, thanks." Amy told her former teacher

about the nonprofit organization she had just started. It was a tutoring service for students who needed extra help but whose parents couldn't afford to pay for it. The ribbon-cutting ceremony would be the next Monday at two o'clock. "Can you come?"

"I would love to," Mrs. Monroe said.

"Great. It's on the corner of Apple and Hickory," Amy said. "Thank you, Mrs. Monroe."

"You're welcome, Amy. And what is the name of your organization?"

"Mrs. Monroe's Schoolhouse."

As Mrs. Monroe hung up the phone, Elmer entered the kitchen, and she beamed at him. Her life had been full and victorious, after all. Teaching was her crowning achievement—and, having inspired one of her students (and, no doubt, others) to continue the tradition in her honor, it was also her legacy. Maybe now Adele could sleep in once in a while and enjoy a quiet Saturday with Elmer.

—*Mikki Hollinger*

In the Light of a Master

The low hum of the bus nearly lulls me to sleep. I look out the window into the eerie blackness of a moonless winter night. It is cold enough outside for the snow to squeak underfoot, only slightly warmer inside. The highway is deserted. It is 4:00 on a Saturday morning. The perfect time, the perfect weather for a warm comforter and a wistful dream. What would possess any sane soul to venture out at a time like this?

When Donna Frenzel recruited me for the debate team, she didn't bother to tell me about the strange weekend hours I'd be keeping. Perhaps she didn't feel it was an important detail. After all, she never seemed to mind it. Year after year, for thirty-some years, she was the first one on the bus. Whether her energy came from (A) her love for tournaments, (B) the time with friends, (C) the six-pack of Diet Pepsi she's consumed, or (D) all of the above, is hard to say. But this morning is no different than any other.

While some students swap the latest, greatest evidence and ideas from recent meets, others try to sleep, despite the bumpy school bus seats and incessant noise. Mrs. Frenzel and her team of judges (mostly teachers) sit in the first four seats. They quickly volley comments back and forth. Laughter erupts like a restless volcano. Then, sudden silence. Someone is passing on a sweet morsel of gossip that's too good to share with too many.

After three hours on the bus, we arrive at a distant school. As usual, we are the first team there. Mrs. Frenzel doesn't like to be late. We unbundle and wait, developing chronic stomach knots as we think about the three grueling hours of public speaking that lie ahead. Mrs. Frenzel seems a bit harried, too. She hands out schedules as she shouts out instructions over the din of the team. Between tasks, she warmly greets fellow coaches from opposing schools. They've become comrades over the years.

The standard "welcome" delivered over the predictably screechy loudspeaker brings conversation to a halt, but the nervous shuffle of briefcases, evidence boxes, and paper continues. "Good luck," says the anonymous voice. Then we're off to test our reasoning skills and public speaking prowess.

When we return to the school cafeteria, it is nearly

noon. We eat greasy take-out pizza while Mrs. Frenzel helps tally scores. She's easy to pick out, boldly flaunting her eccentricities. Her salt and pepper hair is fashionably wild. A huge diamond, a family heirloom, adorns her ring finger. She wears somewhat dated clothes, not for lack of fashion sense or means to buy better, but because they are what she likes. Her pants, crew neck, and vest fall outside the realm of typical teachers' clothes (you know the look . . . cute denim jumper with apple and alphabet appliqués).

Finally, they're ready to announce the winners. We cheer on our novice and junior varsity teammates who take home trophies, while we nervously listen for our own names. I'm sure those around me can hear my heart pounding as they announce the third place varsity team, then the second place team, and finally the winners. It's hard to believe, but we did it. We won! This means we'll be going to the state tournament. Plus, my partner and I both take home a treasured speaker trophy.

Mrs. Frenzel smiles and applauds. She's pleased, but not terribly surprised. She reads the incredulous look on my face. She says nothing, but her look says, *I knew you had it in you. Why are you so surprised you won?* She knows me well.

We board the bus. Everyone's chattering about the day's excitement. Mrs. Frenzel heartily congratulates us all as she hands out the judges' critique sheets. I can see the pride in her eyes. "I knew my girls would win today," she tells us.

At first, in victory's warmth, the miles melt away quickly. But as the hours drag on, the hum of the bus once again nearly lulls my weary body to sleep. I watch the winter sky's muted orange hues being swallowed up by darkness, and I ponder my past three years on the debate team.

In three short competition seasons, I've learned some valuable skills. I can now research issues that concern me, compare information from different sources, and draw logical conclusions. Furthermore, I can comfortably stand before a crowded room and proficiently present my ideas with almost no time to prepare a speech. I am more self-assured, more reasonable, and more eager to take on tough challenges.

I close my eyes in hopes of drifting off, but my thoughts keep me awake. A voice in my head reminds me, *It is not just you. Every single student on this bus, every single student on every other bus for the last thirty-some years, has learned these things and probably a good deal more.*

Then, finally, it occurs to me; I understand. It is not the Diet Pepsi that energizes Mrs. Frenzel (though it probably doesn't hurt). It is her drive to see her students gain all they can from the debate experience. It is her desire to take a verbally clumsy teenager and help him or her perform a linguistic ballet. It is her conviction that the things we gain now will be with us through college and our careers, all our lives.

That is why, for all these years, she's been getting up at 3:00 on Saturday mornings. That is why she ventures out in the bitter cold and darkness when her warm bed is enticing her to stay. That is why, after a full week of work at school, she willingly spends her Saturdays on a noisy, bumpy school bus.

The bus stops in front of our school. After saying my farewells, I pause a moment. I try to imagine who I would be without the influence of this very special teacher. More timid? Maybe. Less articulate? Probably. Organizationally challenged? Most likely. On a different career track? Definitely. But having basked in the light of a master, I now see my path clearly. Maybe someday I'll be an excellent teacher, too.

—*Michelle (Mann) Adserias*

Show-and-Tell

Show-and-tell was not what I thought it would be. But then the whole job was a surprise. I'd submitted my application at the Diocese to teach art, not kindergarten. Why had the principal even picked mine up?

"I have no experience . . ."

"You'll be perfect," the smiling nun who interviewed me said. "After all," she added, glancing down at my application, "You taught that age group in student teaching, you have children that age, and they do a lot of art in kindergarten."

She looked approvingly at my modest attire of a blue-checked blouse and denim wrap skirt. "Now, say the Hail Mary and the Sign of the Cross."

I must have passed her test, even though I wasn't Roman Catholic, because she then shook my hand and said, "Classes start in three days."

When I hesitated, she sweetened the offer by reminding me that my son could attend the school without charge, which, in effect, added quite a bit to my salary and would eliminate scheduling problems. I needed a job, so I accepted.

My first step was to pick up a methods book on kindergarten education from the college bookstore. My second was to consult with my six-year-old daughter, who was an expert, being a recent kindergarten graduate. Both sources agreed that show-and-tell was a must. My daughter informed me it was the best part of the whole day. But when I suggested that show-and-tell could be done at our desks, a look of horror swept her little face.

"No, Mommy, on the rug. Everyone sits in a circle on the rug."

"But there isn't any rug in the room, just a tile floor. They must have gotten along without one last year."

I could tell by the look on her face that that was no excuse.

"I can't afford to go out and buy a rug. Besides, there isn't time."

"They can use my yellow one."

"Are you sure?"

The affirmative nod bounced her red curls. Okay, so it really was important. My Suzie was a great kid, but she didn't part with things easily.

When she saw the large oval rug installed in the

room, she approved of the arrangement of tables, chairs, and toys. I was ready . . . or so I thought.

I had twenty students. Half the children were white, half black; half girls, half boys; half Catholic, half Baptist; and half the Catholics were from an older Russian faith I had never heard of. It would be interesting. Their abilities ranged from those of a little girl who could read any book in the room to those of David, who couldn't even recognize the letter *D* in his own name. Some were well dressed; some had clothes that must have seen the city mission bins several times. One lived in a snug brick home, another lived in an old flat so neglected you could almost see through the walls.

But when we sat in a circle on the yellow rug, all the differences fell away. For show-and-tell, everyone was equal.

"I was run over by a bike. That's why I have a cast on my leg."

"My cousin Christopher has a brain tumor."

"Want to hear the song we are going to sing at the prayer meeting tomorrow?"

We learned about Russian prayers, Baptist songs, and the blow-by-blow account of what happens when your dear cousin has a brain tumor. I found out quickly that the children had a lot of "things" to share. But these things weren't toys, stickers, and pretty stones, as I'd expected. My kindergartners often raised difficult questions, and the answers they wanted weren't written into the curriculum.

"My mom has a baby growing inside her."

"We carry pussy willows instead of palms on Palm Sunday."

"How do babies grow?"

We learned the Hail Mary. We talked about the "fruit of the womb." We talked about fruit and how fruit seeds grow into trees or plants that make more fruit. We looked at apples, saw the seeds inside, and ate the crispy, sweet flesh. We learned that babies grow in wombs, not stomachs, and come from sperm and eggs, which are like people seeds and grow people.

"I went to Christopher's birthday party. He was eight."

Birthdays were celebrated, and when they found out my birthday, they insisted I tell my age, just as they did on their birthdays.

"Thirty-one."

"That's *old*! You're as old as my grandmother!"

They laughed gleefully, and I laughed with them. I was stunned when I did the math, but I had no reason to doubt their accuracy. They knew their numbers and their letters now, even David. And some had grandmothers in their thirties.

"How do babies get out? Will my mommy pop?"

"My mommy was cut. She showed me her scar."

"Does it hurt a lot?"

I admitted it did hurt, sometimes a lot, but that babies were worth it. No, the skin doesn't pop open, even though it might look like it might. We learned there is a special opening where they come out and that babies are not "pooped." Sometimes, mommies did have to be cut, but the doctors made sure the area was numb so they wouldn't feel anything cut them. I answered as truthfully as I could and relieved as many fears as I could.

"Can we sing the alphabet song backward?"

"I'm not sure the song would fit that way."

"You can do it."

I was given a challenge. They had more faith in my musical ability than I did, but after much trial and error, I managed to get the letters to fit with the music. We learned the alphabet forward and backward, as well as the sound each letter makes and how to write it.

We looked at the pictures in our science books.

"See how the mother goose protects her young by leading the fox away from her nest?" I said.

"Yeah, my mom does that when my dad comes home drunk."

"My mom hides me and my sister in the closet when her boyfriend comes over so he won't hurt us."

Understanding murmurs went around the circle. No one was shocked, except me.

"Christopher is in the hospital."

"I can spell 'hippopotamus'!"

Spelling "hippopotamus" turned out to be such fun we all learned how to do it, even David. Then we did a tour of the school, going from class to class showing off our wonderful knowledge. They loved to sing, so I thought it would be fun to teach them the classic hymn with the wonderful refrain, "Jesus loves the little children, / All the children of the world. / Red and yellow, black and white, / All are precious in His sight. . . ."* They were such a diverse group, they would love it.

I had just begun the song when a hand went up.

"They ain't no red people!"

Nods of agreement went around the circle. They knew their colors. A quick comparison of flesh tones followed; dark arms were put against light arms. They agreed: No one was red, yellow, black, or white.

"We are all skin color!"

The children were right. I wished the rest of the world had their wisdom.

We went on to fractions. Dividing one thing into equal pieces was a very easy concept to them.

"That's sharing."

The smiles of understanding glowed brighter than the yellow rug. Fractions were simple. We shared cookies and graham crackers and learned about one-half and one-quarter. It was a good day. Then it was time for show-and-tell.

"Christopher died. They wouldn't let me go see him."

My voice cracked when I tried to talk. I couldn't be the strong, composed teacher; I could only be another mourner. There was no reason to try and hide my feelings from them. Tears dampened the yellow rug, tissues were passed around the circle, and wisdom was shared. I was amazed how much five-year-olds knew about death and how well they could comfort each other. They were quite the theologians.

"Mrs. Edwards, is it true people can come in and take you away from your family?"

"They would get put in jail, wouldn't they?"

"No one can do that, can they?"

Anger and fear swept around the circle; the yellow rug trembled. I hated to tell them that social services could do that, and not be put in jail. Not all show-and-tell discussions were comforting.

On the last day of school I took a picture of everyone sitting on the yellow rug. My daughter had been right: It was important. That circle was the round table where equals met and shared their thoughts—thoughts on social issues, religion, life and death, joy and sadness, the whole gamut of life. It certainly wasn't what I had expected, but I wouldn't have missed show-and-tell for the world.

—*Kathleen Edwards*

*Lyrics by Clare Herbert Woolston

Lizard Boy

I have always believed that my teaching profession would lend me an advantage when it came to parenting. I somehow thought that I would magically have all the answers. I was determined that my child would not be hampered by the stigma of learning disabilities, poor study habits, or uncoordinated motor skills. I suppose having several years of classroom experience convinced me that I was the mistress of educated wisdom.

Every educator is drilled extensively on the varied degrees of learning. We are bombarded by statistics stating the importance of teaching at every child's level. We are encouraged to master the art of varied teaching styles. However, nothing could have adequately prepared me for the task of teaching my own child.

Matthew is a typical nine-year-old boy. He loves fast cars, BB guns, and sports. He even enjoys school, although to admit this would definitely alter his status as the ultimate cool kid. The only thing that mars his perfect little world is his total dislike of anything that remotely resembles reading. He absolutely detests reading. In a household with more than five hundred books, my son's refusal to read has caused me utter dismay. An avid reader, I simply cannot understand how anyone, much less my own child, could not love the infinite magic found between the covers of a good book.

Throughout Matt's first few years of schooling, I simply convinced myself that it was his teachers' fault. They had not done their jobs to instill in him the joy of reading. I couldn't understand why a child who made excellent grades in reading refused to like it even a little. Whatever the reasons for my son's fierce dislike of reading, I decided to find a way to make him fall in love with the wonder of the written word.

My quest took me first to the endless piles of children's books I'd purchased over the years. Together, Matt and I sat on the floor surrounded by mounds of books. We searched for anything that would grab his interest long enough to entice him to read the pages through to the book's end. Our search yielded nothing.

Onward I trudged, frantically perusing the shelves of our local public library. I tried old classics like *Charlotte's Web*. I hopelessly recommended award winners and a whole string of Beverly Cleary tales.

I tried demanding that he read an allotted amount each night. Big mistake. The daily homework nightmares had nothing on the battle waged during the nightly reading time. He moped. He cried. He yelled. Nothing worked.

So, I began reading to him, instead, thinking that if I could just find that one magical story that piqued his interest, he'd eventually seek the book out for himself. I read to him every night for several weeks, after which I encouraged him to complete the book we'd been reading on his own. Zilch. While he enjoyed listening to all of these, much to my disappointment, none of them produced the longing I'd hoped for.

Plan H, or so it seemed, brought me to the conclusion that I had overlooked the obvious. Matthew is an avid baseball player. He plays on three different teams every summer. He eats, sleeps, and breathes baseball. This was it! I knew it! I raced back to the library and checked out as many baseball-related stories as I could find. My results ranged from detailed histories on various Major League players to simple chapter books written for Little League fans. I drove home in eager anticipation.

He caught a glimpse of Mark McGwire and instantly snatched the entire bag of books out of my hand. He sat for hours cruising through one page of statistics after another. He paid particular attention to the photographs and illustrations. He was in hog heaven, and so was I. I gave myself an exhausted pat on the back, thinking I had finally won.

A few days passed before I noticed that he was not actually reading any of the books at all. He was simply skimming through interesting sections, gleaning a little fact here and there. Although he read a few chapters of the novels, it was like pulling teeth to get him to finish any of them. Total frustration set in for both of us. He was sick of my pushing him. I was irritated at not being able to reach him.

I decided to give up. Maybe he would never enjoy reading; maybe it was just a phase he was going through. Though my mother's heart knew it was time to back off, the educator in me found it hard to overlook. I continued to make weekly library visits with him, but I no longer forced him to pick up a book each night. I left it up to his discretion whether he chose to read and for how long.

Matthew recently won a gift certificate to a local bookstore. I eagerly made the thirty-minute drive and allowed him time to comb the shelves at his leisure. Before long, I found myself offering suggestions. He canned each and every one. After a long two hours, all he could come up with was a coffee-table book about the solar system. I suggested we try one more corner of the store. I refrained from forcing my choices. Instead, I asked him what type of story he might like.

"Anything short and not girlie," he said.

He began checking book covers for "cool pictures." After several rejections, he pulled out a small paperback with a funny cover illustration of a gecko lizard and a mockingbird inside a school lunchroom: *Farewell My Lunchbag,* one of several Chet Gecko mysteries, written by Bruce Hale. Chet is a clever, wisecracking fourth-grade lizard detective. Matthew dubbed it his final choice.

I silently hoped this wasn't just another addition to our piles of unread dust collectors. I was shocked when he actually began reading the book right there in the car. He even giggled as he read. His eyes took on a glassy, excited glaze. By the time we got home, he had read over sixteen pages. Hallelujah! He was reading and loving it.

Several weeks and three Gecko mysteries later, he eats, studies, and bathes with a book in hand. He falls asleep with a lizard every night. He walks around the house spouting detective knowledge. No case is too big for Matt Law, master sleuth. While my nine-year-old lizard boy solves the Mystery of the Lost Sock, I am suddenly struck with the notion that he has single-handedly broken the Case of the Fickle Reader and the Paranoid Mother.

—*Christine Guidry Law*

The Beauty Beneath

The South Bronx isn't normally associated with the word "beautiful." The sidewalks are cracked and crumbling and so grimy that even weeds don't have the perseverance to grow there. Discarded newspapers sit at the edges of the pavement, gradually turning to mush. Rusted chain-link fences surround buildings and abandoned lots. The buildings are mostly dingy red brick, with broken windows and cracked and peeling paint. The housing projects rise high into the dusty air, their forlorn and darkened windows looking blankly upon the dismal world.

When I first set eyes upon the South Bronx, I was a first-year teacher, newly graduated from college and looking to do something worthwhile and interesting with my life. Though I had not gone to school to become a teacher, there were a number of programs designed to draw young graduates into teaching in the inner city and I applied to one on a whim. Six months later, I found myself in a classroom in the South Bronx, teaching science to five classes of sixth graders.

Very few teachers have an excellent first year. I was warned many times that the challenges would be many and the free moments few. Teaching is a difficult job no matter where you teach. But there is more than a little truth to the famous slogan associated with New York City: "If you can make it here, you can make it anywhere." It is a city of extremes, harboring the best and worst of everything: culture and commercialism, high society and skid row, intelligentsia and illiteracy, wealth and poverty, crime and compassion.

When my first group of students entered my classroom on that first morning of my first day of teaching, my mouth was dry, my eyes were wide, and a voice that was not my own came out of my mouth. I had no class list and knew no one's name, so I assigned seats randomly and quickly, pointing to a student and then to a desk. I passed out copies of my six-page, neatly typed and bulleted, "Rules and Expectations for the Classroom." We proceeded to go over it point by point, which was my idea of classroom organization.

I can only imagine what my students must have thought. They were rather quiet, not really listening, staring at me curiously, sizing me up. They clearly knew I was a first-year teacher, though no one had told them. They always know, and the rigid presentation of my rules and expectations further revealed my inexperience and uncertainty.

By the following Monday, the kids had formed alliances and had grown bored with sixth grade. Now, they sought entertainment. I still didn't know their names. With four classes of thirty-two students each and one special education class of ten students, I was overwhelmed. There was no personal connection between us. I was merely an adult at the front of the room, yet another authority figure, trying to force them to do things they weren't interested in. They simply ignored me and talked among themselves. When I tried to quiet them, they got louder. Seeing my frustration, a few would speak out loudly: "I'm bored." "You're not teaching us anything." "Make these dumb kids be quiet."

In the midst of this chaos, I would notice one or two students sitting quietly, notebooks on their desks and pens in hand, looking up at me with sweet doe-like eyes. These precious few were the picture of patience and quiet endurance. They were accustomed to this mad scene, had spent six years of school waiting patiently for their teachers to get control of the other students and to teach them something. Sometimes, I would detect hints of their frustration; they would sigh and close their notebooks, put their heads down, stare out the window. The sight of this gentle capitulation would throw me into a silent rage. I felt vexed and guilty at my own ineptitude. And I felt anger at the boorish behavior of the thugs who ran around my classroom, throwing crayons and stealing pencils, punching and tripping other kids, spewing profanities, and raising hell.

I hated them. Still, I tried to do my job well, working long hours at night preparing lessons and writing notes. I tried to think of things that would interest them and get their attention. Each day, my careful planning was trampled, as most of the kids took the first twenty minutes to settle down and then a handful of others would keep up their antics for the remaining twenty minutes of the period.

I tried not to yell, because they usually found it amusing. Using a calm voice, I spoke firmly and tried to put the onus on the student: "You need to sit down." "You need to listen." "You need to stop talking."

One boy continually asked to go to the bathroom, but every time he left, he would wander the halls. One day I told him he was not allowed to go. He followed me around the room wailing and screaming. He dragged himself along the floor, clutched at my ankles, and kicked his feet. I ignored him. He grabbed a book and threw it at the chalkboard. It made a tremendous thud and fell to the floor, spine bent and pages torn. I looked at it as though it were the most boring thing I had ever seen. He got up from the floor, stood two inches from my face, and screamed a stream of profanities at me. Still, I stared back and said nothing. He stormed from the room and slammed the door as he left.

"Well, good riddance," I said and turned back to the chalkboard.

The class giggled, and for a few moments, they listened to me teach.

After only two weeks of teaching, I was frazzled. I'd been getting only four hours of sleep a night, eating only one meal a day, and was under near-constant stress. One afternoon a class came in laughing and chattering loudly, sat down, and proceeded to make noise and ignore me, as usual. I tried to get their attention; they just grinned at me, amused. A few started in with the chants: "Give me a pencil." "I forgot my notebook." "You never teach us anything." "I hate you."

The more I tried to gain control, the harder they resisted. I would get one group of students in their seats and quiet, and another group would jump up and run around, hitting each other, throwing paper, hollering, and pushing over desks. The noise became deafening, and another teacher came into my room to investigate.

They quieted instantly. The other teacher told them that they were acting like animals and that he would call all their parents. He made them pick up their mess and apologize to me for their behavior. Under his direction, they trotted around like puppies, quietly picking up trash from the floor and straightening the desks. He lined them up and marched them out of the room, perfectly straight and silent. As soon as the door slid shut behind them with a quiet click, I burst into tears. I sat on the floor and hugged my knees while I cried like I'd never cried before—a great cloud of misery released in deep sobs and hot tears that went on for nearly twenty minutes.

Over the next few months, I struggled along. I had some really bad days and some not-so-bad days. I called parents of particularly misbehaved children. I wrote names on the board and gave detentions during lunch. I tried to be more confident, more in control. I worked harder at night, sometimes cutting sleep to three hours.

In an effort to engage my students, I tried some hands-on experiments. When we were studying the human body, I brought in a cow heart, and for a change, the classroom was noisy with enthusiasm rather than chaos. The success bolstered my confidence, and I brought in other things for the students to explore: pieces of tree bark, clumps of moss, milkweed pods, and rocks containing small fossils. The children slowly responded, behaving better because they were more interested in the lessons.

Still, many mornings I would fantasize about staying on the subway and never going back to school again. On weekends I was so exhausted that I would sleep through most of the day, lacking the desire or the energy to get out of bed. Sunday nights I would lie awake thinking fearfully of the day ahead. My life was utter misery.

I don't know exactly when the change took place. I'm sure it happened gradually, but I'm also sure there were early signs that I didn't recognize at the time. Then one day in the middle of April, after months of teaching, I looked around my classroom at the students' work up on the walls—brightly colored books about the human body, posters of food webs, diagrams of meiosis and mitosis made with M&Ms and yarn—and I realized that I had taught the kids something. I looked at their mid-term exams, with mostly good scores, and I thought about what they had achieved and the things we had done together. They had screamed with delight when I cleaved a sheep's heart in half and let them stick their fingers into the chambers. They had eagerly picked apart flowers to label the parts. They had giggled while designing and writing stories about imaginary animals to which they'd prescribed a wide array of unlikely adaptations, from spiked toenails to heat-resistant scales. I had laughed many times at their antics and listened to stories about their weekends. Long ago, the black bubble of hatred had melted away.

The "thugs" who had harassed me and cursed me

incessantly at the start of the year were certainly not now model students, but they had stopped cursing. A couple of them even tried to keep order among the others when they chatted too much, barking, "Be quiet. Let her talk."

They talked about their home lives, sometimes sharing stories that were gut-wrenching and heart-breaking to listen to. They spoke casually and earnestly, not complaining or seeking sympathy, just wanting me to know more about them. Many had parents with AIDS, parents in jail, parents who abused drugs or alcohol or them. Most lived in housing projects or homeless shelters or were shuttled among relatives, no one wanting to care for them.

During the last week of school, I realized that I was in love with these children and they were in love with me. They helped clean up my room and pack away my things. The boys showed surprising chivalry and insisted on carrying the heavy things. The girls carefully took down work from the walls and cleaned the tops of the desks. They chatted with me about summer plans and told me that they wanted me to be their teacher in seventh grade.

On the final day of school, my room was overrun with students saying good-bye. They brought presents and cameras to take pictures. They promised to come visit me the following year and thanked me for being nice to them. One boy, known for his cursing and volatile temper, shyly hugged me and blinked back tears.

When you teach kids in the inner city, they are tough on you. Life has taught them not to expect much, and they don't. They have learned to look out only for themselves, and they do. They carry burdens as teenagers that many of us never carry as adults. It is easy to get angry with them, to dislike them for their selfish, horrendous behavior. Sometimes, they make being around them and trying to teach them unbearable. But somewhere deep within each hell-raising student is a child—a kid who needs love and attention and careful direction. You cannot be their friend; you must be their teacher; and in order to do that effectively, you must care about them and want to help them succeed. They won't be perfect children and you might not save them from the streets, but for the time they are in your classroom, they will know that they are loved and they are safe. And they will learn.

The South Bronx is still not a beautiful place. But beneath the grimy landscape, a little beauty does shine through, in the souls of the children.

—Cecilia M. Dobbs

Field Trip

My first school was the storied one-room schoolhouse. An old whitewashed building with a red roof and a vane on the peak, it sat at the top of an unpaved hill surrounded by farmland (including a barn rife with livestock) in a then-unincorporated area of Urbana, Illinois. The school housed all six primary grades and, as I recall, there were about thirty-five of us, mostly very young, although we ranged in age, of course, up to twelve or thirteen.

The year was 1953, and I was six years old, a first grader, and the son of a Ph.D. student at the University of Illinois. My peers and the upper graders were farm kids or children of undergrads taking advantage of the GI Bill. Some were just too poor to live in the city, which would have qualified them for a city school. (I suspect my parents dismissed the relevance of first grade, since most of my education came at home, at their hands, anyway.)

The sole teacher in that school was as classic as the building itself. Mrs. Knapp was a schoolmarm by profession and she'd been doing it, she said, all her life. By then, I'd guess, that meant thirty-five or forty years on the job. She had to have been in her sixties: white hair in perfect array. Petite; memory puts her at barely five feet, perhaps one hundred pounds. Bony, with tightly drawn skin and sharp features. Prominent knuckles. Perfect teeth. She brushed after lunch and made sure we did, too.

She handled our diverse intellects with perfect aplomb, guiding those of us who could read well through the pleasures of Stevenson's poetry and Mr. Popper and those who struggled with reading through the joys of Dick and Jane. If every grade was a different country, Mrs. Knapp was fluent in the six languages we spoke, always having appropriate conversation to offer on whatever subject—academic and not—that our curiosity was heir to. She knew, for example, more about baseball and its history than my father did and was always ready to argue the merits of Pee Wee Reese (her favorite shortstop) against Chico Carrasquel (mine).

The one Mrs. Knapp incident that will always remain engraved in my memory didn't happen at school, however. It happened on a deserted country road that divided cornfields on the afternoon of the last day of that, my first full-fledged school year. To celebrate the beautiful weather, she'd taken us on a field trip, literally, through the bright yellow and green of corn and wheat stalks that were taller than I was (and than she was, too) but still two or three months shy of their harvest.

We wandered, as large groups of children are wont to do, our eyes catching with fascination on every bug and bird and leaf, every one of which, unfailingly, Mrs. Knapp had explanations for. We trekked along utterly untrafficked gravel and dirt roads that had been bull-dozed just wide enough for tractors or a single car to travel. There were no trees: The Illinois prairie land was flat, and we could see only the blue of the horizon and an occasional farmhouse rooftop beyond the fields of grain. We ate our lunch sandwiches along a road-side, listening to the rustle of the wind through the gently waving crops, the cries of the crows, the chirrs of the crickets and beetles.

After lunch we walked more. Now, though, the trip had become repetitious—more fields, more crops, more birdcalls—and I, certainly among others, was becoming impatient. Then, it happened: There, in the absolute middle of nowhere (straight out of what, some years later, I would think of as *The Twilight Zone* or a Stephen King novel), on the side of another single-lane road hundreds of yards from any-thing that resembled civilization, stood an ice cream stand. Nothing fancy, just a wooden counter six or eight feet wide, five feet high, two feet deep, with poles supporting a wood sheet that served as sun cover for the grizzled, but smiling, middle-aged man who stood behind it. The words "Ice Cream—10 Flavors" were painted prominently on the front.

The man and Mrs. Knapp greeted each other as old friends. She turned to us and said each of us could have an ice cream cone, any flavor we wished, her treat. Our enthusiasm was, naturally, boundless, and debate over whether to stick to the known delights of chocolate or vanilla or whether to experiment with the exotic Rocky Road or Blueberry raged among us. But we each settled on something, and the man scooped large scoops into waffle cones and handed them out. We savored and devoured.

Then he asked Mrs. Knapp, "What would you like?" I like to think there was a twinkle in his eyes as he did and that what followed was a ritual between them, although the few kids who'd attended Mrs. Knapp's classes in years before hadn't been to the stand.

She paused thoughtfully, then said, "I think I'll have a cone with a scoop of each."

He didn't bat an eyelash, but we did. *A scoop of each? All ten flavors? In one cone? Mrs. Knapp, this woman who was smaller than the oldest of her students, was going to eat a ten-scoop ice cream cone?*

With the same aplomb she displayed in the

classroom, she took the mountain from him carefully and licked the top. She said something like "Mmm" and smiled. And we watched, agog with envy, as she consumed every sweet mound, moving her tongue up and down from vanilla to strawberry to butter pecan, not losing a drop to the heat of the afternoon.

Afterward, we walked back to the school, perhaps just a mile or so away, packed up our things, said good-bye to her and each other, and walked home or waited for our parents to come.

Of course, I told my parents about the event, and, of course, they smiled. We drove past the school the following week. It was closed for the summer and Mrs. Knapp was off somewhere, with Mr. Knapp, I supposed, eating copious quantities of ice cream stacked in sky-high cones. I never saw her again, and though we looked, I never found that ice cream stand, either.

Now, fifty years later, though the little else I can recall about that first school year is only dimly remembered, Mrs. Knapp and her ten-scoop ice cream cone remains one of my clearest childhood memories. And often, as I watch children sitting in the sun outside modern twenty- or thirty-flavor ice cream emporiums, I wonder if perhaps she isn't somewhere watching, a well-filled waffle cone in hand, still enjoying it mightily.

—*Evan Guilford-Blake*

A Spoonful of Sugar

Early one morning, as the children and I bustled off to church, Pamela, my autistic teen, taught me another lesson on the power of "enthusiasms." *Enthusiasms* is a term coined by Jessy Parks, an artist with autism, to describe the obsessions—or heightened interest in certain things, usually objects—that are characteristic of people with autism. Many therapists try to purge autistic children of their obsessions in an attempt to produce more "normal" behavior. I have found that incorporating Pamela's "enthusiasms" into her therapy, school lessons, and daily life often provide the "spoonful of sugar" that turns drudgery into delight.

As we drove to church that morning, as usual, Pamela latched onto a pencil and the church bulletin and began mechanically recording the years that her favorite videos were released: 1989, 1959, 1950 . . .

Her attention swerved to an article in the bulletin about the origin of Memorial Day, and above the year 1868, she wrote "M" and asked, "What comes next?" Assuming she wanted me to spell either "Memorial Day" or "May," I asked her which word she meant.

"No," Pamela said. "M-C-M-X-L-II, *Bambi*, 1942. M-C-M-L-X-X-III, *Charlotte's Web*, 1973."

Suddenly, understanding flashed in my mind. Movie credits mesmerized Pamela, and by comparing the string of letters shown on the screen with the release date printed on the video, she had cracked the Roman numeric code. But because movies didn't exist until the twentieth century, she didn't know the Roman numeral equivalent of 1900.

I answered Pamela's question, wondering whether she really knew how to interpret Roman numerals. When she then translated several numbers into English, my heart nearly burst with excitement. Once again, Pamela's enthusiasm for the odd and unusual had enabled her to master a new skill, inspiring her in a way that bone-dry explanations in ordinary textbooks usually did not.

I first glimpsed this enlightening deductive process when Pamela was five. At the time her vocabulary was limited to a bunch of nouns, preschool themes (colors and shapes), stock phrases, and piercing screams. Her kindergarten teacher and I were developing goals for the coming year. We noted that, while Pamela recognized upper- and lowercase letters, she had practically no awareness of phonics and poor listening skills. Consequently, her reading readiness had stalled, and we decided to postpone reading instruction until her language had improved. Throughout that year, while we "experts" in education, the teacher and I, wrestled such weighty matters, Pamela quietly slipped into the ring. As she deftly maneuvered through her favorite videos, she connected words to familiar titles of movies. One evening I watched her match video boxes to cassettes, even when no pictures provided clues. Fascinated, I watched as Pamela compared letters on the videos to those on the boxes, one word at a time, and a smile crept across my face as I realized that my daughter was reading.

Pamela gave me a refresher course in enthusiasms the first year my husband and I homeschooled Pamela and her brother. Her lack of pretend play skills worried me a great deal, and I went into red alert when the oddest assortment of objects orbited her play world: a baby blanket, a large yellow Lego window, and a bright orange reading lamp. She rigidly insisted upon playing with these same three toys, in the same spot of our bedroom. Then she dragged the clock radio down onto the floor with her. All attempts to move Pamela to her own bedroom threatened a core meltdown. Nonetheless, I drew a firm line in the carpet when she invited our Kirby vacuum cleaner into her weird circle of friends.

My frazzled brain was unable to unlock the mysteries of her universe until she began to add words began to her play: "Blanky," "Good night, slot head," and "Mr. Loudmouth." The key to this mystery zapped away all my fears: Pamela was re-enacting scenes from her favorite movie, *The Brave Little Toaster*. She had advanced light years in pretend play, for she was well beyond sipping invisible tea from a plastic teacup. Pamela had transformed ordinary objects in extraordinary ways when she cast the yellow Lego as the star of the show, the intrepid toaster. During that year, Pamela donned a soft blue dress, jumped off the top bunk bed, and imagined Alice's parachute into Wonderland. The bunk served Pocahontas well as a waterfall. Pamela's enthusiasms had worked another miracle.

Following her lead, I timidly fell in step with Pamela on these journeys in my attempts to help her learn. Her most despised task, lacing, reduced Pamela to a puddle of tears. Well-worn pages from cherished Disney books breathed inspiration into my brain: I tossed the dull lacing cards in the trash and recycled pictures of her favorite characters into lacing cards with a little help from my poor man's laminator, better known as contact paper. At the debut of her new lacing cards, Pamela's eyes sparked with joy, rather than tears.

A few months later, Pamela staged a minirebellion

against her wheat-free, milk-free diet, forcing me to supply her with an explanation. Most autistic children misinterpret what they hear, and they understand information best when it is presented as written stories. My first attempts at writing nutritional lessons for Pamela were bland and ineffective. So, calling upon Pamela's fondness for repeating cereal commercials, I wrote a story titled, "Why My Cereal Is Just Like TV," soon followed by its sequel, "Why My Food Is Just Like TV." Pamela was so intrigued by the new lacing cards and the dietary stories that accompanied them, she literally ripped them from my hands with anticipation.

Echolalia, the incessant repeating of phrases in a parrot-like fashion that is common to autistic children, can drive parents mad, and I am no exception. In our home, my favorite repetitive phrases, "No more questions" and "No more silly talk," became ineffective defense shields against the tenth consecutive airing of the same question or TV commercial. Lifting a lesson from Pamela's handbook on enthusiasms, I decided to disarm this weapon of Mom's destruction and transform it into an ally. First, I sorted all of Pamela's favorite repetitive phrases into two categories: friend and foe. By playfully adapting the useful phrases into everyday language, I showed Pamela how these phrases (friends) could be changed into sentences to express her needs and thoughts. Completely irrelevant phrases (foes) were sprinkled, like sugar, on top of challenging tasks to melt away tension when Pamela seemed frustrated.

One commercial, in particular, showed great range in academic growth. Pamela loved to sing, "It's Sunday," a promotional jingle for some long-forgotten TV show. This one little tune stretched beyond recognition into lessons in learning the days of the week, months of the year, seasons, prediction of today and tomorrow, holidays, and negation ("It's not Friday."). Instead of cringing when Pamela ensnared a new phrase into her lexicon *du jour*, I started smiling and dreaming up ways to draw echolalia on our roadmap to speech.

Pamela next taught me patience in watching interests take unexpected twists and turns on the road to usefulness. She became obsessed over a newly debuted television show called *Blues Clues* and was adamant about carving a half hour out of our busy homeschooling schedule, twice a day, to watch this show. At first, I resented her demands, but then I rearranged our day and spent that time cleaning the house and filing paperwork. Though the left side of my brain argued that we were losing valuable time to a show that launched reruns from Tuesday through Friday, the right side countered that Pamela's mystifying behavior often produced fruit, so let her creative juices flow. A few months into the show, this the "chipmunk" into a very odd-looking position, smoothing down the ears.

I took a wild guess, "A frog?"

She launched into her victory dance. The final morph of the "frog" was when Pamela removed its front legs, rendering it into a seal. This incident reinforced how enthusiasms, tended with patience, bore fruit.

Pamela and I continue our parallel journeys into the Land of Enthusiams to this day. Lately, she has been conducting a variety of experiments with ice. When I come across icebergs capsizing in our freezer, I wonder what vistas they will reveal to Pamela.

In the meantime, I have started a new language therapy that incorporates things guaranteed to sprout a smile on her face: Beanie Babies, Disney games, pictures of her favorite cartoon characters, and animal stories. In just three weeks, her syntax and sentence structure have become more consistent. She is speaking more frequently in complete sentences, and asks and answers questions with greater confidence.

Now, Pamela actually looks forward to her daily therapy sessions, thanks to the spoonful of sugar sprinkled on top. That gets me thinking about her next lesson: Would Pamela like an inanimate object story about ice, a round-up story about ice piles in the freezer, or a hands-on experience story about making ice?

—*Tammy Glaser*

child who dreaded any activity involving t
paper, crayon, and markers started filling p s
drawings. Why? Because Pamela had spe
precious hours watching the show's characte
draw. Her newfound artistry blossomed int
handwriting, which just happened to be on l
goals for her that year.

Another lesson in patience came about
walked into her room and caught Pamela in t
of snipping a beloved Beanie Baby. I resisted
instinct to rescue a helpless beaver from her
scissors. I hesitated to intervene, partly beca
toy belonged to Pamela, who had no history
posely damaging property or injuring anima
calm demeanor made me wonder whether t
were merely the result of natural curiosity.

A few moments later, Pamela bounced out
room and asked, "What animal?"

I carelessly responded, "Beaver."

Her screams quickly told me I'd failed tha

Then she blurted out, "No, it's a squirrel."

Careful observation revealed the absence
beaver's teeth, and the rodent indeed looked
squirrel. Pamela trekked back to her room, retu
a few minutes later carrying the "squirrel" sans
I quickly ventured that the tailless squirrel mig
a chipmunk, and Pamela's bright smile confirme
accuracy of my answer. Then Pamela scrunche

The Power of One

"Anybody have any questions?" I ask. "How are things going on the playground?"

I'm meeting with our school's conflict managers—forty Asian, Latino, black, and white fifth graders—to practice the conflict resolution skills I taught them a couple of months before. The kids are spread out on the carpeted risers in the school's library, a mini-amphitheatre, looking down on me, an actress on stage. For now, they're quiet, but if I don't keep things moving, I'll lose them.

"Have there been many conflicts to resolve?"

A tall, lanky girl with two braids raises her hand and then shouts out. "A first grader threw a dirt ball at me, so I threw it back."

They've had a few months to get over the excitement of carrying clipboards and wearing oversized navy T-shirts with a gold handshake logo, so today I'm hoping to work out any bugs in the schedule, see what they've forgotten, and role-play the conflict management steps again, if they need it. Apparently, they do.

I love this part of my job as the school psychologist at this urban elementary school, a function of the district's antiviolence plan. Administrators want to cut down on tattling and trips to the principal. I want even more.

When my own children attended a cooperative preschool where I worked one morning a week, they learned to "use their words." I know the power that solving their own problems can give kids. It teaches them much more than when adults do it for them or when they're punished over and over for playground squabbles. Our school's five hundred children are spilling out of the building into portable classrooms on the playground. We have bickering in lines, scuffles over kick balls, and occasional shoving matches to contend with.

"What do we do if the little kids run away from us?" a boy in baggy pants and oversized basketball jersey asks.

Michael's mother is in jail for selling cocaine; his father works two jobs. Michael gets into several conflicts a week—no fistfights yet, but he's come close. He's qualified for the gifted and talented program, but his anger rips out of him like a bomb exploding and I fear he's getting sucked into the cycle of violence we're trying to break. His teacher and I are giving Michael this privilege in the hope he'll learn something he can put to use in his life.

"If they run," he asks me now, "do we chase em?"

With my hands on my hips and my head cocked to the side, I moan. I must have gone over this ten times before. *Maybe it is too late for some of these kids,* I think.

But a boy in the back row answers correctly. "We ask a yard teacher for help."

So, they did hear me.

Then, a petite girl sitting cross-legged in the front row asks, "If the kids hit us, are we allowed to hit 'em back?"

This time I actually pull on my hair. "Hit them back?" I cry. "How many of you think you should hit them back?"

Half the hands go up. A few shout the affirmative. The rest look confused.

"You're conflict managers," I say, my voice rising again. "What do you think you do?"

No one answers.

Another girl raises her hand. "My auntie told me if someone hits me, I'd better hit back."

I know the unwritten rules of their neighborhood. These kids don't live in the roughest part of town, but they still need to stand up for themselves. Unfortunately, that is often interpreted as fighting.

This is not a new dilemma for me, so I tell the kids what I usually say.

"Not at school you don't." I shake my head. "What are conflict managers supposed to demonstrate to the other students?"

I'm met with blank stares and a few tentative raised hands.

"To talk about it," I say.

A couple of them shake their heads in disagreement. "Then we'll be a punk."

"Besides,"—I'm ignoring this last comment for now—"if you hit someone at school, you're no longer a conflict manager."

They know that two students have already been fired this year for getting into fistfights.

"And," I add, "you'll get suspended."

I'll convince them with this threat, I believe, but the girl in the front row speaks again.

"If I get suspended, my mama says, 'Oh, well, you got suspended. At least you hit back.'"

The kids murmur agreement and begin to talk among themselves.

I'm finally silent. I haven't heard this before. I had no idea that suspension was seen as a minor price to pay for saving face. It's a no-win situation. And it perpetuates the violence.

"Why do you think we have wars?" I shout to the group, aware that I might be getting a little carried away. "Because everybody has to keep hitting back."

I have their attention now.

"What's wrong with this? Somebody's got to do something differently. We have to solve conflicts peacefully, with words." We've just celebrated Martin Luther King's birthday, I remind them. "Please just follow the script on your clipboard. Help everybody get along."

Why am I doing this? Teaching kids skills they aren't allowed to use outside of school and, worse, putting them in a bind if they do. At times like this, I feel like quitting.

A week later, Michael finds me on the playground during recess. His conflict manager shirt hangs almost to his knees; he's pressing the clipboard to his chest.

"Ms. Briccetti, I just resolved a conflict!" He's beaming. "These two boys were fighting over the tetherball, and I said, 'Do you want some help solving this problem?' And they said 'Yes,' and I said, 'Okay, what seems to be the problem?'" His voice warbles with excitement, and as he drops his clipboard to his side, I can actually see him straighten, stand a little taller for a minute.

"That's fantastic, Michael! And did they think up some solutions to their conflict?"

"Yeah, they're going to take turns, just like we practiced when you taught us." He's glancing around the playground, either looking for more business or trying to see who's noticing him, I can't tell. "Now, the little kids are following me around the yard, asking if they can help, too." His face is open, expectant.

"I'm proud of you," I say, hugging his shoulder to my side. "Maybe you'll be the one who starts to turn it all around."

He gives me a funny grin, as if he's humoring me, then struts off, clearly back on duty. *At least,* I think to myself, *it's a start.*

—*Kathy Briccetti*

I Speak, You Speak, We All Speak English ...Eventually

I recently taught an adult English as a Second Language (ESL) literacy class that brought home to me a very important point: Teaching is way too difficult a way to earn a living. My next job will be something easy, like mopping up radioactive spills at Chernobyl or teaching cats to come when they are called.

Although I cut my eyeteeth teaching English to beginners, I moved on to intermediate and advanced classes as soon as I could. My year of teaching beginners was a nightmare filled with scissors, magazines, and crayons. I had drawers and folders filled with pictures of everything from fruit to clothing, computers, and firefighters.

I didn't read a magazine or newspaper without a pair of scissors at my side to cut out any picture I might be able to use for the ESL class. I even "liberated" a couple of magazines from doctors' waiting rooms, clipping from them interesting pictures to add to my collection.

Let's face it: It's a lot simpler to explain what a particular fruit is by showing pictures of apples and oranges. Or to talk about clothing by bringing in catalogs filled with pictures of dresses, jackets, coats, and shirts. I suppose I could have pointed to various articles of clothing I was wearing, but I draw the line at showing my underwear.

I spent most of that year literally dancing around the classroom. Officially, it's called the "total body response" method, meaning you use your body to explain things. For example, if you want to explain the difference between walking and running, first you walk and then you run. The same principle goes for standing, sitting, squatting, and jumping. On the plus side, I ended the year in better physical shape than when I started. Of course, it doesn't work for everything, which is why I had all my pictures as backup.

And I may have exaggerated a little when I called it a nightmare, because there were some fun times. Like when I taught my class about verbs having to do with the bathroom, such as "wash," "dry," "flush," and "wipe." Since I couldn't find pictures for some of these verbs, which is probably a good thing, I simply took the whole class into the bathroom and demonstrated the verbs. Well, pantomimed might be a better word. There's a limit to what I'm willing to do for a class.

There was also the time I taught them colors. I had put on green socks that morning, so to show them the color green, I hiked my leg up onto a table, pulled up my pant leg, and pointed to my sock—which was blue. I did the same thing with the other leg, and sure enough, that sock was green. They got two colors for the price of one, and I stopped getting dressed in the dark.

Although beginner students tend to be incredibly appreciative of whatever you do, they are also very needy. I found I would finish teaching a class and be emotionally exhausted. No matter how much I gave, they wanted more. I didn't blame them: They were in a new country and were desperate to learn the language. And I was their lifeline.

But after a year, I "graduated" to higher-level classes and never looked back. Until last week.

A colleague, Kathy Simo, asked me to substitute for her, and I said yes, assuming she was still teaching her regularly assigned level. That's when she gave me the bad news. Instead of teaching high-intermediate, she was teaching level one/two literacy for the summer. So, not only were the students unable to speak English, they couldn't write it, either.

It seems that for the summer session, the school board had temporarily reassigned instructors based on some algorithm known only to board members. Many instructors ended up in different schools, teaching different levels, and basically wanting to kill the people who gave them their assignments as they scrambled to find material for their new levels.

That's how I ended up in an ESL literacy class. Unfortunately, after seven years of teaching higher-level classes, in a rash moment, I'd thrown out almost all of my beginner material. I frantically dug through my boxes of files and found a couple of handouts that might do in a pinch. And this was definitely a pinch.

Most of the learners could write the English alphabet to varying degrees, so it wasn't as bad as it could have been, though there were a few older women who were still struggling with it. Luckily, as a way of saying thank you, Kathy had given me a couple of ideas to try out and I wasn't going in totally unprepared.

Five hours later, I came out dripping with sweat, and it wasn't only because I was teaching in eighty-six-degree weather in a non-air-conditioned school. It was because it's just so damn tough to teach beginners.

Between writing words on the blackboard, holding up pictures, running around the room pointing to things in different colors (color being one of that day's themes), handing out worksheets, correcting students' work, and calming down some of the students who were having problems keeping up, I didn't sit down once. Luckily, I had remembered some of the physical demands of teaching beginners and had worn my running shoes for just that reason.

I came out of that class with two main insights.

One, I gained an increased respect for people with the courage (or need) to leave their own countries and come to a country with a different language and culture. Having spent a summer in a country where I couldn't speak the language, I knew what being forced to point to things because I didn't have the words felt like. In an instant, I was reduced from a fully functioning adult to a child. It was deeply humiliating. While I knew I would be going home at the end of that summer and would instantly regain my adult status, these people were here to stay. For them, there was no going back. For better or for worse, English would be their new language.

Two, I realized that shuffling instructors around has an unexpected payoff. By working with beginner classes, intermediate- and advanced-level instructors gain a new respect for how much work it takes for students to learn a new language. They see the strides students have made in moving from hesitancy to fluency. Conversely, beginner instructors see what they are laying the foundation for; students who could barely put two words together are now using coherent sentences.

As I limped out of the classroom, I was grateful to Kathy for giving me the chance to work with beginners again. I also hoped that she still had some students left and that I hadn't frightened them all away. I called her the next night, and she assured me that she still had all her students and that they had enjoyed my class. At least, that's what she thought they were saying.

It felt pretty good. But not so good that I didn't tell her that if she got sick again that summer, she was on her own.

—*Harriet Cooper*

This story was first published in the Sunday, October 6, 2002, issue of the *Toronto Star*.

A Matter of Trust

I didn't see my own potential until I met Mr. Roach.

You can do anything. You can be anything. You can learn and expand your mind. That was the message I'd received from my dad, but I'd never believed it. Isn't that what a dad is supposed to think about his daughter? It must be a rule in the parenting handbook.

But Mr. Roach mirrored the same message in his own way, and I did believe him. He showed me it was true. He was just my overworked teacher, but he noticed that I needed some guidance in finding my own way.

I met Mr. Roach on the first day of high school. He taught math. Every day for a week, I sat in my chair in the middle of the room. Then came the pop quiz. I was nervous. I hadn't studied before class.

He handed me the paper. It was a breeze. Just

algebra. The sights and sounds of the classroom faded away. There was only math. All I had to do was solve a few equations. The last one was a bit complicated. It was fun. I was the first one done.

I put down my pencil. Time ticked past. I could hear only the rhythm of the clock and the swish of pencils moving across the page, a muted rhythm punctuated by coughs, chair squeaks, and the occasional violent scratch of erasing. I looked around; no one else was finished. Ten minutes had passed. I spotted Mr. Roach sitting at his desk, looking at me as he stroked his beard.

Why is no one else done? I worried. The last question was difficult. *Was it a trick question? Did I get it wrong? Maybe I missed something. Do I have time to check my answers?* I picked up my pencil and double-checked my calculations. I got the same answers. I looked around again, and still no one else was done. Twenty minutes had now passed.

Mr. Roach called time. Groans rose in a wave. I trembled as I handed my paper to Mr. Roach. He barely glanced at it as he grabbed pencils out of the hands of other students. "I said time," he bellowed.

The bell rang. The students surged for escape, sweeping me along. Then I heard Mr. Roach call my name. I turned; the air felt like it had turned to molasses. I saw my quiz in his hand. I froze. I forgot to breathe. My heart seemed to skip a beat and to thump loudly in my chest. *What could be wrong?*

"Meet me in the office after final bell," Mr. Roach said.

Later, when the final bell rang, my stomach said hello to my shoes. I walked to the office. The secretary directed me to one of the counselor's offices. I knocked, and Mr. Roach answered. Inside, another man named Mr. Kirk introduced himself as my new counselor. He and Mr. Roach had been talking about my classes. Mr. Kirk explained that I'd been in the wrong classes and it would take a week to straighten it out.

Mr. Roach made sure I was in the right classes. I don't want to imagine what would have happened if he had not cared. I might not have succeeded academically. However, if that was all he'd done for me, I might have forgotten.

Mr. Roach was my teacher for math, chemistry, and physics. One day in physics Mr. Roach began the discussion of quantum physics, electrons existing at distinct energy levels, probability defining their approximate location within the electron cloud. He said that we could never determine an electron's exact location or behavior. Everything was explained by quantum leaps and probability.

I argued with him. It wasn't true. There had to be a formula. We had one for everything else. I demanded to know the formula. He had to be joking.

Everyone else in class was saying it was easy; you just accept the assumptions. I was embarrassed. He wasn't joking. Still, I didn't want to accept the assumptions. The assumptions upset my sense of order. Finally, I just shut up. A sigh ran through the class. Once again, Mr. Roach asked me to stay after class.

The bell rang, again plunging my heart to the pit of my stomach. *Was I stupid? Why was this quantum stuff so confusing? It just didn't make sense.*

Mr. Roach asked if I wanted to do a special project. Now, my stomach dropped to China. *I was stupid. I needed extra credit.*

"What project?"

"I have one in mind," he said as he stroked his beard. "I think it will interest you. Come to my office after school."

The rest of the day blurred. My mind was numb. After the last bell, I made my way against the tide to the physics/chemistry storage room, which doubled as Mr. Roach's office. Chemicals and glassware lined the walls. Strange equipment with dials and lights sat on the counters. A mixture of chemical smells assaulted my nose: sharp, pungent, acrid. It was not a beautiful room.

Mr. Roach was there waiting. He said, "Glad to see you. This project is just for fun. No grade. No credit. Just for you. For your own knowledge. You can ask me questions here. I'll answer them if I can."

"What's the project? Do I need extra credit?"

"Need credit? You have one of the highest grades in the class. I want you to write a report on Einstein's general theory of relativity."

"I can't do that!"

"Yes, you can."

"I can't figure out quantum physics. How am I going to figure out Einstein?"

"You can do it. By the way, Einstein didn't like quantum physics either."

I spent many afternoons in Mr. Roach's office asking questions. It was the best part of school. I was lucky that I met him my first day. I was blessed that I had him as my physics teacher.

When I turned in my report on relativity, Mr. Roach gave me a greeting card. The card has a picture of Einstein with the quote, "God does not play dice with the Universe." I still have it. It reminds me to trust myself.

—*Mary Paliescheskey*

Last Day

My first year of teaching I taught two classes of seventh graders, and the experience exceeded my expectations. I was in love with teaching.

As the end of the year approached, I became increasingly nostalgic. Having spent so much time with the students, I could hardly bear the thought of the summer without them. I had watched them mature as they dealt with junior high school experiences, such as having more than one teacher, changing classrooms, and having lockers. As a first-year teacher, I had gone through a growth experience myself.

As I drove back and forth to school each day during that last week, I reminisced about the events of the year. I recalled the problems the students had had with their lockers back in September. Before homeroom, I stood just outside my classroom door in case I was needed, watching as the students struggled every morning with the lockers that lined the corridor.

"Can I help you?" I asked a frustrated boy named Dewey who looked like he wanted to cry. Of course, that wasn't possible with his friends watching.

"Everyone has tried to open my locker, Mrs. Walker. I think it's broken."

"What's the combination?" I asked.

Using the numbers he gave me, I narrated the methodology for opening locks as I demonstrated. To Dewey's amazement, the locker opened.

"You are the only one who can open it," he said with admiration.

Feeling necessary and important, I moved on to the next student in need, thrilled with being a teacher and being able to help my students solve their problems.

That last week, I also recalled my small victories, like the time I'd casually written "good" at the top of Debbie's homework. As I passed back the assignments the next day, I noticed her staring at her paper in a daze.

"Is something wrong?" I asked, walking back to her desk.

She pointed at the word I had written. "No one ever wrote that on my paper before," she said.

At first I thought she was putting me on. Then I realized, sadly, that she was not.

"You did a good job," I assured her.

As she proudly showed her paper to the other students around her, I made a mental note to write as many nice things as I could on my students' papers.

Now, in June, I had to say good-bye to the kids I had come to love. I'd grown particularly fond of a girl named Anne. Having skipped a year in elementary school, at age ten, Anne was both the youngest member of the class and the most mature. Every day she would come by after school to chat with me. She amazed me by revealing that she was a fan, as I was, of the poet John Donne.

On those last few days before summer break, I ruminated about the things I had learned that year about children, realizations never discussed in my college education courses. Discovering that many students genuinely disliked school had come as the biggest surprise of all. Because virtually all of my friends and I had loved school, I naively assumed that most of my students would, too.

Luckily, my enthusiasm carried over to the kids in my classroom. They knew I loved teaching them, grading their papers, planning units, and thinking up projects, and they knew I was pleased when they were successful. Of course, not all of my lessons were successful and not all of my students learned to love school. But for the most part, we learned from, enjoyed, and respected one another, and at year's end, I was very proud of how far we all had come.

Having been responsible for these students for nine months, I now felt as though I needed to help prepare them for the summer and the next phase of their lives. I wanted to send them on their way with good memories, sound advice, and a warm good-bye. To that end, I painstakingly composed an insightful, uplifting farewell speech.

So, I wasn't at all receptive to the advice I received from Jeanie Lizer, my department chairperson, on the day before the last day of the year. I had just dismissed my morning class and was heading for the faculty room for lunch.

"Bonnie, we've got to talk," Jeanie called to me as I passed by her door.

As I waited for her to catch up with me, I wondered what I had done or hadn't done to warrant her serious tone. Perhaps my book count hadn't balanced or I had forgotten to complete one of the year-end reports.

"I need to say something," she said, hesitantly. "Let me tell you about my last day of school the first year I taught."

"Everything's been going fine," I interrupted. "I'm not having discipline problems."

"No, that's not it." She paused, then quickly spit out the words. "I don't want you to be hurt."

She had my attention. "Hurt? Hurt, how?"

"You love those kids, and I know you. Tomorrow you'll be standing up in front of the class giving a teary speech, and they'll be throwing confetti and cheering as they run out."

Jeanie had me pegged exactly, but I was immediately defensive. Seeing my reaction, she tried a different approach.

"Look, you're a good teacher and the kids like you, but they'll run out anyway. It's not personal. I just want you to be prepared, that's all."

We had reached the faculty room door by then, and the opportunity for private conversation had passed.

"Okay," I said. "Thanks."

Although my emotions and state of mind had been obvious to Jeanie, until that moment, I was unaware of them myself. Hot tears filled my eyes.

"Are you okay, Bonnie?" Jeanie asked.

"Sure. I'm fine."

Jeanie continued on to the ladies room, and I went into the faculty room. I got my lunch from the refrigerator and a soda from the machine and choked down my food. When I returned to my room to meet with my afternoon class, I was uncharacteristically quiet.

The ungrateful little so and sos, I thought angrily, scowling at the students I had loved all year long. *They won't miss me for a minute.*

Seeing their smiling faces, hearing their chatter

about their summer plans, I suddenly realized that Jeanie was right. If it had been the last day right then and the bell had rung that moment, I would have yelled, "Good riddance to bad rubbish," and slammed my roll book shut to show them that I didn't care one bit if they ever came back to my class.

When the bell rang, signaling the end of the day, I coldly announced that they were dismissed. Debbie hung back to find out what her final grade would be for the year. Finding me unusually unreceptive, she soon left.

Well, next year she will have new teachers to hang around, I thought bitterly.

On the way home from work that day I revised my farewell speech. The new one was designed to separate myself from them with the least amount of pain. *Could it be true that they would never think of me again? Sure, most of them would forget me. I expected that. But not Debbie, whose confidence I'd helped boost. Not Dewey. Not Anne.*

The next day soon arrived, and I braced myself for the worst. I got through my morning class by striking a pose of strictly "business as usual." The students and I played a game of Password with the science vocabulary words we'd collected during the year. I stood between the players in front of the room, moderating as I had done dozens of times before. Everyone was eager to take a turn, even though they were no longer getting a grade for their work. The students loved this game and had the words, the definitions, and even the winning clues committed to memory.

A few minutes before the bell rang and before they would leave for the last time, I saw my chance to take a break from the game. Despite Jeanie's warning, I was determined to make a farewell speech.

"I've enjoyed having you this year," I started, then stopped to fight the lump in my throat. Before I could compose myself and say more, the bell rang and they all let out a loud cheer and dashed out of the room—exactly as Jeanie had predicted. That short sentence was my entire speech. I wasn't sure how many, if any, of the students had even noticed it.

I stood alone and pathetic, front and center in the room where I had held court all year. My entourage had fled. Only Anne hung back.

"They are not very mature," she said sympathetically, reading me like a book. "I hope you have a wonderful summer, Mrs. Walker."

"You too, Anne."

"See you next year," she said, giving me hope that my affection for my students had not been all one-sided.

I took a deep breath and readied myself to repeat the whole farewell process with the afternoon class, determined to be tougher. I was alone for only a few seconds before the students bounded in, talking animatedly to each other. Watching them, it occurred to me that these boys and girls who had entered the room as scared twelve-year-olds nine months earlier were now relaxed, self-assured teenagers, laughing, joking, and looking forward to the carefree days of summer.

I started them on a game of Password. I smiled to myself when I saw Clarence, one of my problem students, already asleep at his desk. When I spotted a chance to make my farewell address, I managed to get through two sentences before I choked.

"I hope you all have a good summer," I said. "I have enjoyed getting to know each of you."

Then, the bell rang, waking Clarence. Within moments, they were all gone. The last day of my first year of teaching was over. Like all true loves, I will never forget it.

—*Bonnie L. Walker*

Moment of Truth

Mrs. Vancleave is wearing my least favorite outfit today: a matching skirt and blazer. The pattern, little checks of navy blue, white, and lime green, makes my head spin. The texture and awful colors make it look like she ripped up an old polyester sofa from Goodwill and sewed together an outfit just for the sake of looking ugly.

"Class, if you would open your books to your assignment, we will go over it. Today we will check our own work."

I pick up my tan wooden pencil and begin scribbling along the edges of my workbook. As I mark the ones I've missed, I realize I haven't done so well on this assignment. I cover my page and glance around to see how many other little hands are flicking their pencils each time they miss an answer. My thoughts are jumbled as Mrs. Vancleave breaks in.

"Class, please correct your mistakes."

The room echoes as rubber meets the paper and eraser dust flies. I quickly correct my mistakes, undaunted by the thick lead smudges I leave on my paper.

Mrs. Vancleave teaches the next lesson and then hands out math worksheets. She walks back to her desk. I hear the sound of her desk drawer opening— the sound that can mean only one thing at this moment: *stickers!*

Behind me now, Mrs. Vancleave is talking to my classmates as she slowly walks from desk to desk, but it is only a faint murmur. I crane my neck to see today's sticker. *Oh!* They are marvelously beautiful. And they are as big as my hand. They are big, bright hot-air balloons, and I want one.

Suddenly, the murmur becomes a clearly audible chant as my wonderful sticker opportunity gets closer and closer.

"Did you get your answers right before corrections?"

My stomach sinks and the room slowly fades away as I look down at my paper only to see clearly corrected work with traces of scraggly pink eraser marks. As if in slow-motion surround sound, I hear the adhesive peeling smoothly from its home onto the workbook's rough page and Jason Gregory's grubby little hands and stubby fingers smoothing on the sticker, making a slight squeak.

My despair begins to lift, and I feel a slight tingly sensation as my body fills with anxiety. Mrs. Vancleave is right behind me. I can smell the old, musty polyester of her ugly suit. I poke the longest nail on my left hand to my teeth and begin to chew, carefully considering my options.

Before I know it, Mrs. Vancleave is at my desk and I can see right before me the sticker I have lived my whole life to take home. Her words become a pounding drum of noise, and without thinking, I open my mouth and a fast, high-pitched "yes" jumps out of it. With a rush of heat from my toes all the way up my spine to my earlobes, the sticker is mine and the ordeal has ended. She didn't even look at my paper.

Once again, my stomach sinks as I look at the shiny hot-air balloon. It's not even the one I wanted.

I stuff my workbook back into my desk and get back to work on my math paper. There is a big origami-like owl on the paper and pictures of over-sized nickels, quarters, and dimes lined up to be counted and calculated.

I turn around and look at Mrs. Vancleave. She has taken off her blazer to reveal her short-sleeved, navy blue silky shirt. I watch her put her reading glasses on the tip of her nose and hunch over her grade book. I try to focus on my math problems, but my stomach hurts and my head is foggy.

I look around to make sure no one is watching, pull out my workbook, and walk the seven feet to Mrs. Vancleave's desk. She looks up at me through her old-lady reading glasses as if to say, *Can I help you?* Hot tears fill my eyes and, before I know it, begin streaming down my cheeks. I blubberingly explain to her that I lied.

I wait and then watch in horror as my exceptionally wise teacher peels that hot-air balloon off my paper, tearing it in the process. Mrs. Vancleave reaches down and again opens that exciting drawer of stickers, pulls out a sheet of yellow smiley faces (the scratch and sniff ones), and delicately affixes one to my paper.

"There," she says. "That's for telling the truth."

She hugs me sweetly, ugly outfit and all, and I make my way back to my desk, completely oblivious to the stares, tears, and snot.

I am on top of the world.

—*Tanya M. Showen*

The Other Two Chairs

We were two chairs short, so we sat in a circle on the floor. Twenty pairs of eyes—big, round mud puddles that went to unfathomable depths—stared at me in concern. The kindergarten classrooms were overflowing, and each of these children had been ripped from their teachers two months after the school year had started and deposited in an empty room on the third-grade hall. My room. I galloped into my new—and my first—classroom, as Demeter, ready to gather all the children to my bosom to suckle knowledge.

My first reality check came when I arrived and found the room completely barren. Where were the decorations, the chalk for the blackboard, and my teaching assistant?

I had planned the lessons for the first two weeks, assuming I would be provided with the materials common to a kindergarten classroom: crayons, paper, paint, easel, books, chalk, tables, chairs. All my room had was a chalkboard and a set of building blocks.

I soon discovered that even if I'd had the materials, the children didn't have the background knowledge to follow my lesson plan. They knew no colors, no letters, no shapes. They were like the blank chalkboard at the far end of the room. I wanted to cry.

Desperate, I sat with them in a circle on the floor and began by asking each child, "What's your first name?"

Five of my students couldn't answer, because they could speak no English. One of them didn't even know her name.

"Little Mama," she answered when I asked her.

I blinked.

"Her twin's name is Big Mama," Mario added. He was the only English-as-a-second-language child in my class who actually spoke English.

"No," I said, once I got the cotton out of my mouth that shock had stuffed into it. "Your name is Ashley. In here," I pointed my finger downward, "you will be called Ashley."

Little Mama, who was one of the few students who did speak English, looked at me as if I was speaking Martian.

Once we had gone around the circle and heard,

at least, most of their names, I went around the circle and invited each child to share with me and their classmates anything they wanted to talk about.

"What's your first name, teacher?"

"My momma whooped me this morning for hitting my sister."

"I know when I'm gonna be nine; that's when my daddy gets out of jail."

"Miss Edwards, we got a hole in our window. A bullet went through it."

"Ain't it true that Jesus loves everybody?"

So, I told them my first name, and I talked about not misbehaving at home and how one must be careful with guns and that, yes, Jesus loves everybody. I knew I was walking on dangerous ground, talking about religion in a public school. Scenarios kept running through my head of the vice principal coming into my room and catching me in this illegal and unprofessional act.

At the end of the day, I approached one of the other kindergarten teachers. "Where is the supply closet?" I asked.

She showed me. In it was construction paper and bulletin board backing. Nothing else.

"Where do I get my class supplies?"

She looked at me for a long moment. "Didn't you bring your stuff from your internship?" she asked.

I shook my head. "It belonged to the classroom."

"It belonged to the teacher," she said.

I started to cry.

As I drove home, in the quiet of the car, the full impact of the day hit me. *What am I going to do?* I thought as I fought panic. I had no materials, no mentor, no assistant, no experience, and no idea what to do with these children. I couldn't just talk to them all year. I felt duped.

When I got home, my mother was appropriately shocked. "The school gave you nothing?" she asked over and over.

Already incensed at the size of my paycheck, this fueled the fire for her. I had remained at home because I didn't make enough money to move out. Now I had to cannibalize what little income I made to stock my room.

"Don't worry," my mother reached over the kitchen table and patted my hand. "We'll come up with something."

That weekend my mother and I sat and made things for my classroom. I relied on file folder games, matching games, pieces of games made from coloring books, anything that could be made quickly, easily, and cheaply. I arrived early Monday morning and began hanging decorations and teaching aids around the room.

The weeks passed, and still I was given no assistant. The children used my homemade materials, but I had a hard time keeping them in working order. Often, a game would be destroyed when more than one child wanted to play with it. A tug of war would ensue, and before I could get to them, it would be torn.

In December, the flu made its rounds among the third graders and eventually crept into our classroom. One day only four students showed up, brought in by their parents.

"He wouldn't stay at home," said a mother. "He wanted to come to see you. Wish I could get my other four to feel that way."

That day we played housekeeping all day and drank chicken soup.

In March, I found a bird's nest. I put it in a plastic box, like the kind you buy cupcakes in at the grocery store. It became our centerpiece of conversation for weeks.

"Did that come from a tree?"

"Why aren't the baby birds in it anymore?"

"How do they keep that together?"

I went to the public library (the school library was a graveyard of books more than a quarter of a century old) and checked out all the children's books I could find on birds. I read to my students about migration, nest building, and regurgitation. We made nests out of twigs we found on the school grounds. We painted colored birds with the watercolors and construction paper my mother had bought for the class and hung them from the ceiling.

During math centers one day, one of my students, Mario, came up to me. He held up an egg carton counting game. Three had been torn earlier that week. Now he held up another broken one.

I snatched it from him. "How did this happen?" I yelled.

Mario's face reddened. "Me and Sergio were playing—"

Before he could finish, I threw down the egg carton in a rage. I closed my eyes, stomped my feet, waved my fists in the air, and shrieked like a banshee.

A third-grade student from next door popped her head into my open door. "Miss Edwards?" she asked, her face a mask of fear.

"You stay here," I said through clenched teeth. I stormed past her and went outside.

I walked around the school for twenty minutes, fuming silently to myself. *I've worked so hard. I've made so many things. I've done so much. And no one appreciates it. Who's to appreciate it? The kids? Of course, the kids.* But as soon as that thought formed in my mind, I calmed down. *They're five years old, and I am acting like a two-year-old.*

Upon returning to my classroom, I found the third grader had the children sitting in a circle on the carpet. "Thank you," I told her, feeling thoroughly foolish. "I can take over from here."

"You sure?" she asked. "Because my teacher said that I was to stay here until you were better."

I laughed. "I'm sure, sweetie."

I sat on the carpet and looked at the kids. The children looked at the ceiling, the carpet, the wall decorations. "I didn't act very kindly just now, did I?"

No one said anything.

"I shouldn't have acted like that," I told them, looking at each of their faces in turn.

Still, I could get no eye contact.

"I was angry, and I didn't think," I said, feeling like a fool. "That's no excuse. I was wrong. I'm sorry."

All of the children raised their heads and looked at me in stunned silence.

Ashley cocked her head to one side. "You're sorry?"

"Yes," I told her. "I'm very sorry. I understand if you're angry with me," I addressed them all. "And it's alright for you to be angry with me."

"You're sorry?" Ashley asked again.

"Very sorry," I whispered.

All twenty children rushed at me and engulfed me in hugs.

The children stopped talking about "whoopings" and visiting parents in jail. Following our unit on birds, one of the children found the shed body of a cicada. They were as enthralled with it as with the nest, so we began a unit on insects. After that lesson, one of them pointed to the slide on the playground.

"There's a triangle," he said.

"Where?" I asked him.

"There," he pointed again, throwing his arm in the direction of the slide. He moved his finger, out-lining the slide, the ladder, and the ground. "That's a triangle."

That launched our unit on geometry.

At the end of the year, nineteen of my kinder-gartners could write their full names. Ashley knew her name was Ashley. All my English-as-a-second-language students spoke functional English. All twenty of my students had advanced between one and three years developmentally—a higher growth average than any other class in the school. My growth was immeasurable. We never did get the other two chairs.

—*Katherine L. E. White*

Extra Credit

Diana had scraped knees and wore a too-large-for-her-body dress created from feed-sack calico when she entered the school on the country road outside of Macon, Missouri. She hung her cape on the peg, got a drink from the crock with the spigot, and carefully replaced her cup on the hook. Plucking her books from the green-plaid satchel, she went in search of her desk. It wasn't hard to find, being the smallest one and yet so big for this tiny child that the teacher, Mrs. Miller, had placed a wooden soda case on the floor next to it to use as a step so she could climb into the seat. In this one-room schoolhouse, one teacher taught all eight grades.

Later that morning, Mrs. Miller stopped at Diana's desk. "Read me your lesson," she said.

Diana picked up her blue reading book.

"'See . . . Dick . . . run. See . . . Spot . . . run. See

. . . Dick . . . and . . . Spot . . . run. I . . . see . . . Dick . . . and . . . Spot. Run, . . . Sally' . . . uh . . . uh . . ."

"Sound it out," coached the teacher.

"'Sssa-id . . . sssa-add. Said'!" Diana said with glee.

"Yes, Diana," Mrs. Miller said with a resigned sigh.

"I read all the words right, except that last one. I sounded it out without help." The child's eyes pleaded for understanding.

"But you're pausing between each word. You need to make your words go faster, like this: 'See Dick run? See Spot run? See Dick and Spot run?' Then the words flow smoothly, not all choppy like you said them."

Diana hung her head. "I'll try to do better."

Diana practiced, and she improved somewhat. When she was called on to read, she could read about three or four words without a pause. "'See Sally fly . . . a kite. Dick . . . likes to . . . fly a kite, . . . too. When Sally runs . . . Spot runs, too.'"

"No," Mrs. Miller said. "Stop making those pauses. Read it again."

Diana read it again, in the same way. Mrs. Miller shook her head and frowned. Whether she meant to or not, she was sending the child a message: *You're no good at reading.*

Diana got the message. *I'm a poor reader,* she told herself, internalizing the perceived negativity. She began to dread storytime, when the children had to read aloud.

The following year, a new teacher came to the little schoolhouse. When Diana was asked to read, she said, "I am not a good reader." Then she read in the choppy manner to prove it. The new teacher's stern face seemed to verify Mrs. Miller's verdict.

Diana lived far out of town on a farm. Every week her parents took her to the library and allowed her to check out seven books, one for each day. She read and read. She read every book in the series about children from other lands and the biography series of the men and women who pioneered the American West. She read other series about the lives of the American presidents and their families and about wild animals and how they lived. Diana knew a lot of information, and she read well when she read silently, to herself.

But she still could not read well aloud. She stuttered, she stammered, she lost her place, she left out entire lines of text. She hated it. So, she became adept at not getting called on. She learned never to make eye contact with the teacher and never to look out the window and appear distracted, either. She learned to hold her finger on the correct page and to leaf through the book with her other hand so that it appeared she had not yet located the proper place.

Usually, the teacher, seeing that she was not ready, would call on someone else.

Diana was placed in a Catholic school for her middle years. She hoped her new school would have teachers who could help her. The nuns did made suggestions: "You seem to keep losing your place, Diana; run your finger along the line that you are reading." That seemed to help some, but she still stammered and paused between words and phrases. Sister Mary Lawrence gave her an index card to hold on the line she was reading, but that met with no more success than the moving finger.

When she stood to read before her classmates, she was doomed. As she stumbled over the words, she could hear their snickers.

"You did fine; don't worry about it," her friends said.

But the boys were not so kind. "Oh, Lord. Not Diana again. 'The stars are . . . spaced in the sky . . . in a regular . . . pattern,'" they mocked.

As she stood to read, sweat popped out on her brow. Her face reddened. She could feel her cheeks blush scarlet with shame. With every episode of poor reading, she grew more and more self-conscious. She tried various ways to get out of reading aloud.

Diana knew she had to participate in classes, so she became agile at raising her hand during English, history, math, religion, and science. Every time the teacher asked a question, she wiggled in her seat, thrusting her arm up, ardently seeking eye contact with the teacher. She waved her arm with eagerness until the teacher called on her, and then she dominated class discussions until the teacher would finally say, "All right, Diana, put your hand down now. Let's give the others a chance to contribute, too."

"Okay," she answered with relief, knowing she was now off the hook for the next subject—reading.

The overzealous-class-participator routine in conjunction with the eye-contact-avoidance technique she had perfected in primary school normally worked to stave off being asked to read in class.

Then she graduated to high school, and she had classes with different teachers in different rooms. There, her carefully designed strategy of eye-contact-avoidance and classroom-discussion-hogging became obsolete. She was doomed. Teachers called on her to read aloud. She stumbled through the readings, humiliated.

Kaye Robnett taught freshman social studies. She always had the pupils read sections of the chapters aloud. Diana dreaded her class. When Diana first got up to read, she told Mrs. Robnett, "I am a poor reader."

Mrs. Robnett nodded in acknowledgment and said, "Let me be the judge of that."

Diana read as usual, cheeks burning in humiliation. The rest of the week, Mrs. Robnett asked her students to stand by her desk to read. On Friday, Mrs. Robnett asked Diana to stay after class.

Diana was mortified. After the other students left, she blurted in anger, "I told you I was a poor reader."

Mrs. Robnett laughed and said, "You are not a poor reader. In truth, you are too good a reader."

"Too good a reader?" Diana echoed in disbelief

"Yes, when I ask the class to read supplemental materials, you are always the first one done. When I quiz you, you always know the answer. So, you clearly have excellent reading and comprehension abilities. Far from being a poor reader, you are the best reader in the class.

"When I asked you to stand by my desk," she continued, "I watched your eyes. They were darting back and forth, back and forth as you were reading. Diana, the problem is that you are reading faster than you can speak. There is a big difference between silent reading and reading aloud. The solution to reading better aloud is to slow down your eyes.

"Here, try it," she said, thrusting a book into Diana's hands.

"'Jefferson Barracks was founded . . . in 1828, becoming the Army's first permanent base west of the' . . . uh, I'm sorry . . . 'Mississippi.' That's better, isn't it? Oh, my gosh! This is too good to be true!"

Diana resumed reading: "'Fort Bellefontaine, north of St. Louis near the confluence of the Missouri and the Mississippi Rivers, was frequently innundated with flood waters, which caused' . . . uh . . . 'the Army to relocate the fort.' Oh, Mrs. Robnett! That was better, wasn't it? I was reading better, wasn't I?"

"Yes," Mrs. Robnett answered, smiling broadly, "you read very well. Now, practice, Diana. Just read slower so you can speak the words before you forget them and lose your place."

Overcome with joy, the young girl laughed out loud and gave Mrs. Robnett a big hug. Thereafter, the teacher and student shared a special affection all through Diana's high school career.

Diana went on to college, married, had a family, and moved to the St. Louis area. Her parents died, severing her ties to the tiny town of Macon. When her husband left the marriage, Diana raised her children as a single parent, returned to college, and earned her bachelor's degree and then a master's of fine arts in creative writing.

She was invited back to Macon for her fortieth high school reunion. A former classmate, Mary Anne, phoned and said, "Come on, you've still got family here—mine. My sister, Paula, has invited us to stay with her. We'll ride on the homecoming float and have lots of fun."

So, Diana went. By then, Mrs. Robnett was in a nursing home at the edge of town. Mary Anne and Diana volunteered to bring their former teacher to the alumni dinner, but Paula said that arrangements had already been made for others to bring her. She explained that Mrs. Robnett had developed Alzheimer's disease and suffered from "sundowners."

"Sundowner's?" Diana asked.

"Yes, it's when old folks do pretty well during the day, but after the sun goes down and their bodies get tired, they become easily confused and agitated. So, it is better that somebody with whom they are familiar cares for them."

At the reunion, Diana went over to Mrs. Robnett's chair and took her hand. "I'm Diana Angelo," she said. "Do you remember me? You taught me how to read aloud well."

"Why, I did no such thing," Mrs. Robnett said crossly. "I was never a reading teacher. I taught history and social studies."

"Yes, you are quite right," Diana said, "and you were a wonderful teacher."

Mrs. Robnett looked at her blankly and then brushed her away. "I want to talk to Paula," she said.

Diana moved aside and watched. Though she was sad that her old teacher did not remember her, she took comfort in knowing that Mrs. Robnett remembered the job she had done so well and for so long. She had, indeed, taught history and social studies . . . and much more.

Her former pupil, Diana, is now the assistant director of admissions at the University of Missouri-St. Louis. On behalf of the English department alumni, she is frequently asked to speak to various groups on the subject of creative writing. Whenever possible, she obliges and reads aloud from her own work.

—Diana Davis

I Can't Read

A red-headed boy was struggling with tests in my sophomore woodworking class. Pat was one of my most enthusiastic students, and I wondered why he was having so much trouble. I discovered the cause of his problems one day when I asked him to check a posted message in the attendance office and to report the information back to me. He walked slowly out of the room and came back in a few minutes.

With tears in his eyes, he said, "Mr. Malsam, I will do anything for you, but don't ask me to read anything." He lowered his head and confessed, "I can't read."

I could hardly believe that he had progressed to the sophomore year of high school and not learned to read. Apparently, he had managed to get through school by memorizing the teachers' words in the classroom and verbally repeating them back. I don't know how he was able to complete the written work and tests necessary to pass his academic classes, but I suspect he was simply "passed on."

After I discovered he could not read, I had my student assistant read the multiple-choice test questions to him at test time and circle the answers he gave. If I had the time, I sometimes pulled him aside and read the test questions to him, scoring his test answers on the spot. No homework was required in my woodworking class or in any of the other industrial arts classes at Westminster High, which made it easier for him to make good grades in those courses.

Over the next two years, I learned more about Pat as he continued to take my industrial arts classes. He told me his father had been an electrician and that he'd seen his father accidentally electrocuted and killed. Pat was only five years old at the time.

I wondered whether the trauma of seeing his father die and the difficult years that followed, at a time when most kids are learning to read, might have caused or at least contributed to Pat's reading deficiency. I'm not a reading teacher or a school psychologist, though, so I didn't attempt to analyze and resolve the problem. I just tried harder to teach Pat more about woodworking. He was an eager learner and earned As in my classes and in other industrial arts classes, but he continued to receive poor grades in his academic classes.

One summer, I took Pat and my son on a fishing trip in the mountains. Another time he went with us on an overnight trip to gather wood in the mountains. We became friends, and I think I became somewhat of a substitute father for him.

His widowed, working mother, unlike some of my other students' parents, always attended his parent-teacher conferences. She repeatedly thanked me for helping him succeed in his school work.

At the end of his senior year, Pat had managed to earn enough credits to graduate from high school. Every year before graduation, teachers in each department select an outstanding student in their academic area. These students, along with scholarship winners and outstanding athletes, are recognized at a special senior awards night. The teachers in our industrial arts department agreed that Pat should receive the outstanding industrial arts student award, because he had demonstrated remarkable improvement and proficiency in all his industrial arts classes. Not only was Pat adept in these classes, he was also very good at assisting other students and helping them set up machines safely. Some of the school's counselors, having earmarked Pat as a slow student, objected to giving him the industrial arts achievement award. We insisted that his name be retained on the list for our award, and it was.

At the ceremony, after all the students had received their awards, Pat suddenly stood up. "I can't sit here any longer. There is something I have to say. I haven't gotten any scholarships, but I have earned a high school diploma like everyone else. I never would have gotten this far if it hadn't been for one teacher who took extra time to work with me and who encouraged me when I became discouraged in other classes." He paused. "That teacher is Mr. Malsam."

Teachers, parents, and students applauded his impromptu speech. I was stunned at receiving the unexpected public recognition and surprised that this shy young man had the courage to speak so eloquently. It was one of the most rewarding moments in my twenty-seven-year teaching career.

The story doesn't end there, however. The next morning before school started, the principal said to me, "In all my years in education, I've never seen a student stand up and speak so truly from his heart."

"I would like to do one more thing for this student," I said.

"What's that?" he asked.

"I want to help him get a job," I said. "The head carpenter in our school maintenance department is retiring. I think Pat would do his job very well. He would make a dependable employee for the school district. He has the ability, and he's trustworthy and hardworking."

After I'd convinced the principal of Pat's skills for the job, he called the maintenance supervisor. Pat was offered the job right after graduation, and he has proven to be an outstanding employee. He does his job well, and he is respected and liked by his coworkers.

When Pat got married, he invited my wife and me to his wedding. At the reception, he proudly introduced me to his guests as his favorite teacher. A few years later, Pat used his carpentry skills to build a lovely home on country acreage for his new family.

It has been nearly twenty years since Pat stood up to praise me at the senior awards ceremony. I'm retired now from teaching, but he still occasionally calls or stops by my home to see me. I don't know whether he ever learned to read after graduating from high school, but I suspect he learned minimal reading skills on the job. I do know that he continues to work enthusiastically and capably as the school district's head carpenter.

As educators, we don't always succeed in turning around every student who has problems. Nor can their success—and ours—always be measured by how well a student scores on academic tests. Sometimes, the best we can do is to help a student succeed in life. My part in Pat's success makes me feel very proud of being a teacher.

—*George Malsam*

The Joy of Learning

By the age of fourteen, I had basically accomplished nothing, save to vilify myself to the teachers at Mather Junior High School. I had deliberately become every teacher's worst nightmare. With relish, I disrupted each class I entered, not caring about the consequential detentions or a suspension.

That all changed the minute I walked into Mr. Kaplan's social studies class. Young and handsome, he was leaning against the chalkboard with his hands stuffed in his jeans, as if he hadn't a care in the world. But his steely blue eyes, shaded by a swath of sandy blond hair, said otherwise. This cool teacher in his Calvin Klein jeans and tan V-neck sweater had a look that said, *Don't mess with me.* Definitely interested and a bit intimidated, I decided there and then to behave myself.

"Good morning," he greeted us, then pushed

away from the board and began to walk the aisles between desks. "My name is Mr. Kaplan, and we are all about to embark on a journey."

Feeling a flutter in my stomach, I wondered if I might be sick, then realized it was excitement. Smiling to myself, as Mr. Kaplan returned to his desk, I felt a spark of hope that maybe this class would be fun.

Suddenly, Mr. Kaplan jumped on his desk.

"Listen to me," he demanded, as if we could do anything else. "This is not about school. It is about learning and the joy it can give, if you let it.

"This is about you," he said, jumping down from his perch with the grace of a panther. "And you," he said, pointing to various students as he repeated the phrase over and over.

When his long, graceful finger settled on me, I thought my heart would burst. Never before had I believed there was joy in learning. Never before had I considered that learning might be about me.

Then, in a hushed voice, barely above a whisper, he said, "History is a mystery, and we are all part of that mystery."

You could have heard a pin drop in that class.

"We would not be here today if our ancestors had not fought for their beliefs, for their independence. We certainly would not be free," he declared with such seriousness that I felt duty bound to hear him out.

Balling up his fist passionately and holding it

before him, he continued. "Every one of you has a history. We have a responsibility to remember those before us and to learn from them."

I had to stop myself from screaming, "Hallelujah!"

"Now, I ask all of you to join me on this journey of life. I ask you to dare to enjoy this journey. If you can handle that, stand up and move your desks to the edge of the room."

It was a challenge. He was asking us to actively participate in his class, not just while away the hour. Within minutes, the room was cleared.

"Now," he said, "I want you to lie on the floor side by side."

The previously silent room erupted into giggles as we clustered together on the floor. Elbows and knees touched and a few heads banged, but we managed to fit together in a haphazard shape.

Once we were quiet, he spoke again, rubbing his chin and looking at us as if we were his latest art sculpture. "Good, now move in closer."

Again, we laughed as we squeezed tighter. Soon, though it was fun, we began to feel uncomfortably cramped and hot.

"Good," he said, as he paced around us. "Now, imagine being chained to one another in a room so small you can barely stand up in it and with only a tiny slit for a window. The heat is so stifling it makes our New England summers seem mild.

"Imagine being fed slop at the end of the day, if you survived the day's heat, stench, and beatings. Imagine sleeping sandwiched together on a hard floor, as you are now, practically on top of each other.

"Imagine that nightmare," he said, his eyes gleaming with righteous indignation.

I wanted to scream.

Then, with the seriousness of a dying man, he said, "That was how the African slaves felt as they were being transported in the bottom of ships to America, only to be sold, after their arrival, like live-stock at auction and then worked nearly to death on plantations. You see, the nightmare you are enacting here on this floor, free to get up and walk out of this class, was only the beginning of the never-ending nightmare of slavery."

That's when it hit me: Mr. Kaplan was teaching us. Without boring books and tedious tests. I was learning. And it was only the first day.

So it went, day after day, week after week. One day we were on our desks crossing the high seas on the *Niña, Pinta,* and *Santa Maria.* On another we were fighting the Civil War with our army contingents and paper rifles. On another we came dressed for the signing of the Declaration of Independence. I was John Adams.

I learned a lot in that class. Oh, we read books and took a few tests, but because we had so much fun, I didn't mind and did well. I looked forward to class, not just because Mr. Kaplan was young and handsome and cool, but more so because he was an outstanding teacher who actively engaged us in the learning process. I respected him, and when he told us that all subjects are important in the journey of life, I made an effort to attend all my classes and looked forward to coming to school.

My parents were ecstatic and wondered at the magic of this teacher who had transformed their wayward daughter into a model student. Parents, students, fellow teachers—everybody loved Mr. Kaplan. Especially me.

So, when rumors started to circulate that Mr. Kaplan was being fired for repeatedly ignoring the school board's request to stick with the curriculum, no one believed it. Mr. Kaplan was the best teacher in our school. Why would anyone fire a teacher who made history real and memorable to his students, who taught them to love learning?

But we soon learned the rumors were true. Mr. Kaplan was bucking the system, a system that measured a teacher's performance by adherence to a formula, to a prescribed curriculum, and to students' successful regurgitation of certain facts, rather than on what students had actually learned and understood and retained. What mattered to the school board was not the quality of the teaching, but the method of teaching, and Mr. Kaplan's teaching was unorthodox.

When it was announced that he would be leaving, all the students and many of their parents protested, to no avail. Always the optimist, Mr. Kaplan took it in stride. He encouraged us to "embrace change," because, he told us, those who cannot inevitably hurt others as well as themselves. Although we knew he was right, we were not about to sit quietly and watch him leave. It was Mr. Kaplan, after all, who had taught us about our ancestors fighting for what they believed in. So, the eighth-grade class hatched a plan to walk out on Mr. Kaplan's last day. Everyone was sworn to secrecy, but word leaked out and soon the principal was giving warnings over the intercom that anyone caught walking out of school or planning a walkout would be suspended indefinitely.

The day finally dawned, and when the bell rang for lunch, everyone in the eighth grade put down their books and headed arm in arm for the front doors. Soon, the seventh graders joined us, leaving the school virtually empty of students. As we made our way outside and to stand beneath the second-floor window of Mr. Kaplan's room, teachers pleaded with us to stop this nonsense and consider the consequences. But Mr. Kaplan had taught us about consequences and the bravery required to make a stand.

We ignored their warnings and chanted as loudly as our voices could carry:

"Keep Mr. Kaplan! Keep Mr. Kaplan!"

Parents showed up, and instead of reprimanding their children, they linked hands and formed a wide circle around the students, chanting right along with us. Local news stations appeared and interviewed some of the students. Then, Mr. Kaplan appeared at his window, tears streaming down his face. He waved at us, mouthed the words "Thank you," and stepped away from the window.

The noise died down as we all stood transfixed, staring up at the window, wondering where he had gone. For a moment, I wondered whether we had done the right thing. *Was he upset with us? Was he proud that we had taken a stand for what we believed in?* My answer came moments later when Mr. Kaplan, dressed in his Sitting Bull costume and headdress, appeared in the window and spread his arms wide to encompass us all.

One of the students raised the American flag on the flagpole, shouting, "Mr. Kaplan rocks!" The crowd erupted into cheers. At that moment, I fully understood another lesson Mr. Kaplan had taught us: I had the power to change and the ability to affect others.

Despite all our efforts, Mr. Kaplan was fired. But due to the overwhelming support of parents and the local news stations, none of the students were suspended.

Mr. Kaplan took a job in another state with a new school run by parents. These "charter" schools are very popular now. Whenever I hear of one, I think of Mr. Kaplan. And I give thanks for this extraordinary, dedicated teacher who took risks and used his knowledge, creativity, and humor to give some dull-eyed students the gift of a lifetime: the joy of learning.

—*Jacqueline D. Cross*

Mama Mentor

Karen sat forward in the uncomfortable office chair, long brown hair falling in her face as she squirmed slightly. She looked ill at ease when I asked what I could do for her.

"Well . . . um."

I was surprised at her hesitancy. On the first day of class she'd glanced through the syllabus and announced, "I hate *Jane Eyre*." No lack of confidence there. As I remember it, I shot back, "You won't after you've read it with me,"—faking all the way. She was a seventeen-year-old first-year student; I was thirty-two and in the first year of my tenure-track job.

In my office, she finally got to the point. "I'm here because I want your life."

I leaned back in my chair, startled. My four-year-old daughter was having night terrors. My spouse was finishing his dissertation, fighting the depression and isolation of writing three thousand miles away from grad school friends and colleagues. I was finding my department a little less congenial than it had appeared at recruiting time; my attempts at humor fell flat, and other junior colleagues appeared preoccupied and angry. I didn't say any of that to Karen as she went on.

"I've always wanted to be a professor and to have a family. And I've never known anyone, before you, who had that."

There it was. Somehow, unwittingly, I'd become a role model.

Nine years after that first conversation, Karen was well on her way: all-but-dissertation in a respected graduate program, in love, and starting to talk, concretely this time, about marriage and family.

The subject came up when we met at a mutual friend's commitment ceremony. We stood in a dimly lit, cavernous room that was decorated for a wedding. Dance music pulsed as I shouted over it.

"If you're ready for marriage and kids, Karen, you might want to think about starting a family in grad school rather than waiting."

I told her about a recent newspaper article on having children in graduate school and about my own experiences.

"I took my orals six months pregnant with my

first child, my daughter, and was on dissertation fellowship when she was born. In some ways, it was the best maternity leave in California."

She laughed, a bit uncertainly.

"I wrote my first chapter when my daughter was a few months old, putting her in day care for between ten and thirty hours a week, depending on how the writing was going. That kind of flexibility was great for us both. But I had to be back in the classroom when my second child, my son, was six weeks old. It was a lot harder. I went back to work brain-dead and sleep-deprived, and even if my students didn't notice—and I'm sure they did—I felt it."

She asked about leave policies, nannies, extra time to degree versus time on the tenure clock. As the sounds of a wedding swirled around us, I mentored my first academic daughter.

She's not my daughter, of course, and that's part of the pleasure. I've never had to discipline her, make her eat her vegetables, or choose a school for her. Nor has she ever given me a mother's day gift or a cold. Though Karen is not my daughter, I am a mother, and that's a part of my identity that I've never hidden, in the classroom or the office.

Not every teacher can share a private life in the classroom, of course. Karen's and my conversation took place at the commitment ceremony, as it happens, of another of her mentors, a colleague of mine.

This woman is childless by choice and a rising star in her field (which is Karen's, as well), an obvious career role model for Karen in some ways. Her partnership with another woman was a cause for celebration to which she'd invited only a few former students; others might never know. My more conventional choices are far easier to turn into classroom anecdote, my status as professor of women's studies softened at times by my status as married mother. *She can't be a radical feminist*, students assume. Yet, combining teaching and mothering the way I have may be the most radical statement I could make.

When I got home that evening, hoarse from carrying on our conversation over the cranked-up sound system, I felt a twinge of envy for Karen. More than a dozen years before, when I was about her age, I'd informed my childless dissertation director of my first pregnancy, by letter to her sabbatical home in France. I'd written as many drafts of the letter as I had of my dissertation prospectus, finally choosing to share the news with her in the context of my topic, family relationships in nineteenth-century novels. We never spoke about my family, beyond her perfunctory congratulations when my daughter was born, yet my dissertation topic invited discussion of family relations. My undergraduate mentor was, indeed, married with children, but he never brought them into conversation, so I hadn't known how to.

These teachers taught me, by word and deed, that professionalism was incompatible with parenthood— that I had to choose, and, implicitly, that mother- hood would be second choice.

Unlike my own professors, I've brought my chil- dren to class when their school was out and mine wasn't. Both children have sat through classroom discussions, more than once joining in (to the great amusement of my students). Last spring I taught "The Owl and the Pussycat" to a classroom full of children's literature students, accompanied by my five-year-old son chanting along with the rhyme. I've taught while becoming increasingly more visibly pregnant, both times finding that some of the insights of feminism seemed more real to my students as they watched my body change in front of them. And I've used anecdotes about my children and my life to illustrate the points I make in teaching. How better to make the point about the feminist implica- tions of naming, for example, than to bring up my own conflicted decision about changing my own name when I married? Temperamentally unable or politically unwilling to compartmentalize the various aspects of my private and professional lives, I have unwittingly modeled a kind of life for my students that I never saw while I was in school.

So, I envied Karen that she had me as an under- graduate mentor, someone in a different discipline, unlikely to sit in professional judgment of her. I can give advice freely, without the disguised competition or power games that sometimes arise between mentor and student in the same field. I can speak as someone who has done some hard time in the trenches and can point out the pitfalls. And Karen has not only me, but also my colleague as well as other female professors with other lifestyles, modeling other choices.

My female professors during my undergraduate years were few and far between. I believe I took two courses, in my four years, from female professors. I recall admiring one glamorous German professor from afar, knowing I'd never achieve her seemingly effortless ease, her nearly ruthless intelligence. Add in graduate student teaching assistants, and I get a few more, but I recall pitying, rather than envying, those odd ducks, who, themselves, were confused as to whether they wanted to make friends with us or serve as authority figures for us. I never knew whether any of them, the professors or the TAs, had children or life partners, or whether their lives were difficult or pleasant, or whether they'd made any compromises. I now wonder how hard the German professor was working to make her life seem so effortlessly glamorous. Is it possible she had spent sleepless nights comforting crying children before coming in to talk to us of Robert Musil and Herman Hesse? If so, at what cost?

I had to make up my life as I went along, assuming that the victories of feminism were permanent, that somehow I could "have it all." When I couldn't, when it became too difficult or complicated, I let it show. If the personal is the political, after all, the reverse is also true, and I could teach that message better when I enacted it. My students and my children have seen much of that, and will continue to.

My own daughter is thirteen now and says firmly that she has no intention of being a college professor. But if she were to follow me, I'd want her to know Karen and women like her—women who can mentor without losing credibility, who can both mother and teach and know they aren't the same, though at some sweet times they resemble each other.

—*Elisabeth Rose Gruner*

Innocence and the Divine

My mother has been a teacher for as long as I can remember. Out of the many stories she has told about her life as a teacher, one in particular never fails to make me smile.

Back in the early 1960s, she taught at a small school in the country. The school served grades one through twelve, and I would be surprised if the total number of students ever reached four hundred. It was a simpler time, a time when paperwork was a minor irritation and some of the largest joys came from the smallest voices.

Though this school was not large, it did have one distinction: It was one of the first schools in the area to get an intercom system. Not a sleek, desktop model with digital displays and wireless capability like the ones today. No, indeed. Remember, this was the early sixties. We hadn't set foot on the moon yet, and color TV was still just beyond the horizon.

The intercom was powered by a huge panel that took up an entire table. The microphone was an industrial gray tabletop model that probably weighed three pounds. Each classroom had its own speaker, connected to a toggle switch on the control panel, so the principal could send messages to individual classrooms or, by throwing the master switch, to every room simultaneously, as the need arose. The teachers could respond and subsequently be heard on the large speaker mounted next to the control panel in the office.

Oh, the joys of modern technology.

My mother was teaching there when the system arrived. It was installed over the summer break so that everything would be ready when the students arrived for the new school year.

Toward the end of the summer, some of the teachers headed to school to prepare their rooms. They put fresh chalk and new erasers in the chalkboard trays, cut reams of colored paper to make bulletin board displays, checked supplies, arranged books, and took care of the hundreds of last-minute chores that precede the coming of a new school year.

During that same time, a few of the cafeteria workers came in to make their back-to-school preparations, seeing to it that the kitchen was set to start churning out peanut butter and jelly sandwiches, soup, and those lemon sheet cakes that have fed millions of students over the years. While the kitchen preparations were underway, a little girl named Mary wandered over to my mother's classroom to read while her mother sorted, scrubbed, and double-checked the supplies.

Mary's mother worked in the cafeteria, and since my mother always had shelves full of books in her room, it provided the perfect place for a little girl to sit and read while everybody finished their various chores.

About midafternoon, my mother went to the office to pick up the list of students coming to her class in the fall and to gather from the supply cabinet a few additional things she wanted for her classroom. While she was in the office, Mary's mother spotted her and came inside to say hello.

"Judy, I hope Mary hasn't been any trouble for you. It was nice of you to offer to let her stay in there with you. Lord knows there's a lot a child can get into in that kitchen."

"She was fine," my mother said. "No trouble at all. She has just been sitting in there reading, not bothering a soul. She even helped me put up one of the bulletin boards a little while ago. When I left, she was stapling the border around the edge."

They talked a while longer, and then Mary's mother said she had better go to the room and get her daughter so they could head home.

"You don't have to go down there and get her. We can just call her on the intercom, and you can wait for her here."

Both women looked around. The principal had been working with the intercom system while they were talking and he was putting the finishing touches on what would become the school's first "command center." Although it was wired and ready to use, he was still putting labels on the control panel. Each label had a number representing the corresponding classroom. There were additional labels for the cafeteria and the auditorium, and even a pair of outside speakers.

"We can do that now?" Mary's mother looked at the table full of 1960s space-age technology.

"Sure," said the principal. "We'll just switch it on, let it warm up a minute or two, and flip the switch for room 212. We need to test the system, anyway, so, now is as good a time as any."

He turned the large brown knob on the side of the panel, and a low-pitched hum filled the room. The amber glow visible through the seams in the panel indicated the tubes inside were heating up. After another minute, he flipped the switch for my mother's classroom, and the test was underway.

"Mary."

The principal grinned and waited for her to

answer. A few seconds passed, and he flipped the toggle switch again, keyed the mike, and tried again.

"Mary."

A half-minute passed, and still there was no response. The principal asked if Mary might have left the room to go look around, and her mother assured him she would not leave the room and just wander around.

The principal flipped the switch once more, leaned close to the microphone, and increased his volume.

"Mary, are you in there?"

Five seconds passed, and then a small voice answered.

"Yes, God."

Oh, for the good old days.

—*Thomas Smith*

Piranha Class

I t was a heady experience, sitting there, watching them work, an isolated observer in a mass of quiet pens scraping across paper. At times like these she sensed a strange suspension of the passing minutes, as if she could somehow pull each student to her privately and talk at length, without a gap in time or production, as the others blindly focused on their own writing. But the illusion never lasted. A few exquisite, analytical seconds more, and the first papers would start rustling, students shifting their adolescent frames uncomfortably in the cramped desks. She glanced at the clock. Quizzes must be taken up now or group discussion would be a farcical exercise in speed. But the students seemed so intense.

Quizzes, grades, bureaucracy. She wished, not for the first time, that she could ignore the details and just teach them to write, to think. Lunch detentions, bathroom passes, parent calls. Tell Andy to write that book; help Rich to piece together, albeit painfully, one paragraph of his thoughts. Equipment requisitions, pep rallies.

The first day of class they'd told her they couldn't think. Remediation, honors requirements, scope and sequence, departmental meetings. "We can't do all that stuff you're asking us to, Dr. Reed. You're too hard; we're just dumb kids." Fire drills, assembly schedule, homecoming. "We didn't have a good teacher last year." (They'd harassed the poor guy out of the teaching profession.)

The piranha class, fistfighting, jumping out of windows, uncontrollable. Family breakups, alcohol, drugs. What was American Lit against that?

"You can think," she'd told them, "and I'll prove it to you. Here's your first assignment."

And she'd graded them as if they could do the work, writing messages in the white spaces beyond the red-ruled lines of their papers, answering their complaints with challenges.

"Define *boring*," she wrote. "Then give me three examples from the text to support your reasoning."

Slowly, out of the anger, out of the fear, they wrote. They wrote about things they couldn't talk about, about people who died or perhaps who should have, about running away or being in love, about being scared and confused and not admitting it.

"The part in the hospital is really strong," she wrote in the margins. "Go with it—your reader needs to understand what happened the night your father died."

She looked at them now and forced herself to call time, to refrain from crushing them with her acceptance. "It goes against everything in my personality to tell you to stop writing," she said, scanning her lesson plan. "But all I wanted was to make sure you'd listened this week."

She passed by each desk, casually collecting papers, allowing desperate, scribbled sentences to conclude just as she arrived.

"I wanted to write more; I just didn't have enough time." This, from the girl who'd implied early in the year that a one-page homework assignment was a vicious plot to keep her from experiencing her young life.

"You're going to like this one, Dr. Reed."

Knew you could do it, Rich.

A top honors student glared at her. "There is no way we can give you a decent analysis in only five minutes, Dr. Reed."

She smiled. They'd had fifteen.

Unexpected agreement rose from the class.

"We had examples from the text."

"Who could support opinions so fast?"

"I wanted to talk about the main character's philosophy of pain."

The teacher sat down in an empty desk, a little giddy. "I've succeeded," she said slowly.

The students watched her cautiously. What new trick of authority was this, then?

She looked at them in something like wonder. "The first day of school you argued with me because I expected you to write, to think. Now you're frustrated because you want to write more, think more, give more than I require you to." She lifted her arms over her head in a kind of bemused victory sign. "That means I've done what I set out to do. I've taught you to think on a deeper level. I'm a success."

The class stared indulgently at the odd person that fate and the administration had placed in charge of their class. Behind her, someone said, "No, it just means you didn't give us enough time for the quiz."

—*Cheryl Reed*

Walk Softly, Children Working

The early morning rush hour has begun. Buses, motorcycles, and cars crowd a busy street in Guatemala City. Men in business suits and women in the latest fashions stride purposefully to work. Along the sidewalk, shoeshine boys wait hopefully for customers.

Roberto's torn jeans are tied at the ankles with strings. One string has slipped and is cutting into his flesh. His bare feet are pushed into worn cotton shoes. A customer sits on Roberto's rough-hewn wooden chair. His knees already throbbing as they push into the uneven sidewalk, Roberto places the man's foot on a small stool and snaps the plastic protector around the customer's ankle, guarding the cuff of the man's slacks. He scoops up the black polish with his fingers and quickly applies it to the man's scuffed shoes, as the shoeshine boy next to Roberto calls out, "*Tsch! Tsch!*" trying to attract businessmen to his chair. As Roberto pulls the cloth back and forth to bring up the shine, he hears his little sister crying. His grandmother is pulling the little girl back onto the sidewalk.

A bus, belching a cloud of exhaust, pulls away from the curb to join the four lanes of traffic. Roberto's grandmother returns to her juice stand. She deftly peels oranges and squeezes them in her metal hand press. Two large glasses of juice, covered with plastic, stand ready for thirsty customers. The carton of eggs on her table is for those who prefer a raw egg in their morning juice. Roberto's little sister, clutching her grandma's skirt, is weeping. A raw red cut beside her eye is swelling rapidly.

Antonio, wearing a colorful shirt and a hand-woven jacket, stops near the little girl. He gently touches her head.

"She was playing on those metal poles and fell into the street," the grandmother calls to Antonio over the traffic din.

Antonio nods. He puts down his briefcase and looks around for Roberto. The two exchange a silent grin. While Roberto's customer pays him, Antonio opens his briefcase. It is filled with pencils, crayons, papers, and articles. Roberto shakes his head "no" to another prospective customer. Antonio squats down on a bench as Roberto hoists himself into his shoeshine chair. Antonio hands Roberto an article to read, about pollution in Guatemala City. Roberto holds the paper, momentarily focusing his thoughts. Then he begins to read, mouthing the words silently. When he has read the article three times, Antonio gives him a paper and some pencil crayons.

The teacher and student exchange a few words. Roberto bends over the paper for ten to fifteen minutes and then hands it to Antonio.

"Write your name and grade," says Antonio.

When Roberto hands the paper back to his teacher, Antonio shows it to me. A slow smile of pride crosses his face. On the paper, a huge cloud of exhaust almost hides the cars and buses and, on the street, a small boy, thin and shivering, is having trouble breathing.

"He got the main idea," says Antonio, and with utmost respect, he puts the paper into his briefcase. He shakes hands with Roberto, saying, "I'll see you tomorrow at the same time."

Antonio teaches some of the thousands of working children on the streets of Guatemala. He is allowing me, a teacher on leave from my job in Canada, to follow him for a few days as he teaches. Last week, I walked in the main garbage dump of this huge city. I saw lovers stealing kisses among the stench of rotting refuse, the only home those young people have ever known. I went to large markets and saw many other young children who work ten hours a day, six days a week, selling fruit, begging, peddling cheap jewelry. And, tucked away in unused corners, I saw teachers, like Antonio, gathering these children together for an hour a day, or twenty minutes a day, giving them a chance at literacy, at an education.

We move on. Antonio walks half a block. Behind a small peanut stand are a girl, about thirteen, and her father. Antonio shakes hands with both and speaks briefly with the parent. Then he turns to the girl. "We'll start classes today."

"Now?"

"Right."

The girl pulls out two plastic containers from under her table, stacks them one on top of the other, and sits on them.

"She's in year three," says Antonio.

Her writing assignment is: *Think about one thing that is really difficult in your work. What can you do to change it? What have you done? Did it work? Why or why not? Do you need the help of someone else? Who? What could that person do?*

A short time later, we move on down the street. At the next corner, an extended family has two stands, one of fresh fruits cut and packaged in plastic bags and another of electronic equipment. The three boys here are more rambunctious.

"We're starting today? Where do we sit?"

"Today, we'll do a dictation."

The single chair becomes a table, and the boys quiet down as they kneel around the chair and labor to write. . . .

> *Today is January 12. Most schools began today. I looked out of my window this morning and I saw many children getting ready and walking to school. They seemed happy. I got up early too. But I got ready to go to work. I also have a right to happiness. I also have a right to an education. Today, I, too, will start classes.*

Antonio moves on. We walk into a tire repair shop. Through the back door I can see a boy of eleven, stacking old tires. The owner calls to the young boy. He and Antonio sit on the bench in front of the counter. The boy has never held a pencil, has never been in a classroom. Antonio hands him an 8½-by-11-inch line drawing of a tree and asks him to trace it, first with his finger.

"Which hand will you use?" Antonio asks.

The boy looks down at his hands. "The right one, I think."

Antonio hands him a yellow crayon. "Now, follow the outline without lifting the crayon from the paper."

Next, he does the same thing with a red crayon

and then a green crayon. Finally, Antonio produces another paper. On it is a cartoon face—an outline that swirls off into the word "*yo*" ("I"). Tiny drops of perspiration form on the boy's nose as he carefully follows the loops and curves that will later lead him to print letters and words. Conversations in the shop quiet down. After twenty-five minutes of intense work, the boy goes back to his job of stacking tires. He shakes the stiffness out of his wrist and grins slightly. The owner looks at the boy with pride and, as the boy passes, he puts an arm around his shoulder.

This deceptively simple program is giving thousands of working children in Guatemala a chance at literacy and empowerment. When the everyday challenges of my job and the difficult circumstances facing some of my students threaten to overwhelm me, I think of Antonio and the street children of Guatemala. I remember the poverty and their struggle. I remember the makeshift classrooms and impromptu lessons. I remember the students' thirst for knowledge and joy of learning. I remember their parents' pride and perseverance. I remember the ingenuity and dedication of their teachers. And I am humbled and inspired.

—*Madeleine Enns*

Truth and Consequence

I t is 7:00 A.M. on a New England summer morning, and Chris Moore is standing in the dewy meadow with a tape recorder slung around his neck, holding a satellite microphone toward the trees.

"*Caw, caw,*" his reedy voice calls out, followed by, "*chickadee dee dee dee, chickadee dee dee dee.*"

He carries on this way for a couple of hours, and I watch with admiration while he chats with the birds hiding in the trees. When the heat of the day becomes unbearable, we leave the meadow and head back to the lab.

Someone once pointed out to me that if you rearrange the letters of the word "education," you get the words "action due." This story is my act of gratitude due to Chris.

Chris Moore, Ph.D., professor of psychology and

animal behavior, was really into birdsong. His particular interest was mockingbirds and other song-
mimicking birds.

"One night, I was lying in bed and I heard a car
alarm go off," he once told me. "I got out of bed and
went to check on my car, but the sound wasn't
coming from there. I guess I should have known that,
since I don't have a car alarm and my nearest
neighbor is almost a mile away. Anyway, I'm
standing out in the driveway in my pajamas, trying to
find the source of the sound."

From beneath his wildly long set of eyebrows, his
eyes widened with suspense. "Eventually, I looked
up, and there, on top of the garage, glowing in the
moonlight, was a mockingbird, singing the car alarm
song," he said, and then whistled the familiar tune.

"Now, think about it," he went on, snapping
back into his teacher's voice. "If a bird's song is supposed to communicate something, how does a mockingbird talk with other mockingbirds if it's always
mimicking other birds or crickets or car alarms? And
why on Earth does it take them so long to say what
other birds say in just a quick chirp?"

To unravel the mystery of the *Mimus polyglottos*,
Chris obtained a research grant and stocked his
office with thousands of dollars' worth of computer
and sound recording equipment. And Chris—a fifty-
year-old professor who grew his own vegetables in an

organic garden, wore the same outfit every day, and always carried a Leatherman—became the most technology-savvy professor on campus.

Chris's theory about mockingbird song was that the information was contained in the patterns of the notes, not in the notes themselves. So, the message in the song "*a b a b*" was in "*a b*" repeating; "*a*" and "*b*" had no meaning on their own.

Students who were interested in animal behavior came to do research in Chris's office, now renamed "the birdsong lab." Like any academic research, the plan was to test a hypothesis and publish the results in a scientific journal. Every professor knows how important published papers are to receiving funding and tenure. We assumed it was the same for Chris.

I joined the birdsong lab during the summer after my second year of college. That summer, I spent twenty-five hours a week listening to about eighteen minutes of mockingbird song. The tape recordings had been converted to digital sound files. Chris and I would sit at the computer, looking at sound waves, playing single minutes of song over and over, listening to a single note at one-tenth the normal speed, and whistling birdsong back and forth to each other.

In the mornings, I would listen for Chris's arrival, the sound of his limping gait and whatever obscure Broadway show tune he was singing that day. We started the day with a chat, usually about animal behavior, while he drank his morning latté.

"Do you know why monarch butterflies are poisonous?" he would ask. "Because they eat poisonous food."

He told me why clovers in Ireland grow with different numbers of leaves (something to do with the fact that sheep eat clovers one leaf at a time), and he told me about birds who steal the nests of other birds, sometimes pushing the eggs right out of the nest. Once he showed me a paper he had written on survival of the fittest as seen in a bowl of alphabet soup.

Chris's was not a typical college professor's office. A large Persian rug that had belonged to his father covered the grey industrial carpeting, and all the clocks were one hour slow, because he refused to follow daylight savings time. ("A grand example of the human race's ability to delude itself," he called it.) On the wall hung a framed needlepoint with the message, "I feel your pain," meant as a jab at psychoanalysis, and, tacked up in the dog days of summer, a newspaper clipping of a blizzard with the message, "Lest We Forget!" scrawled across it. I loved it there.

Sometimes at lunch, Chris would share his homegrown sugar snap peas while he explained various statistical analyses. We would marvel together over the patterns that were emerging out of the birdsong samples. I would whistle for Chris the different patterns of song I'd identified, and he would proudly hang my data analyses in the office suite hallway. At some point we began discussing the plan for the next semester; my stay had become more than a summer stint.

That fall Chris and I attended an academic conference on animal behavior. I was too naive to be shy at the time, so Chris stood aside while I presented a poster on our research findings, whistling mockingbird song to smart-aleck graduate students and wise old professors. Later, we went for lattés and ice cream. Driving back, we talked about family and our childhoods. He told me about his father, who had first instilled in him a love of birds when he was a young boy, and about his wife and children and the farm they lived on in western Massachusetts. We became friends.

A few months later, I left to spend a semester abroad in London, England. I told Chris I'd be back that summer, and with a happy glint in his eye, he agreed to hold a place for me in the lab. By the time I returned, enough headway would have been made for us to start preparing a manuscript.

But when I returned, the birdsong lab was the last thing on my mind. For four months I'd worked as an intern at a London museum, the longest stretch of time without classes or homework in my life. After tasting that freedom, the thought of school filled me with dread. There was no way I was going back—not for the summer and perhaps not at all. Teary eyed, I explained to Chris that I wouldn't be back for summer research. Instead, I opted to work two jobs at local greasy spoons.

Soon enough, though, the autumn breezes came, carrying the scent of academics and falling leaves. I returned to the birdsong lab, glowing with goodness and intent on doing a senior thesis on mockingbird song.

"So, the prodigal daughter returns," Chris said.

We went for lattés and discussed the research plan. He was quieter than usual, and I silently wondered why he didn't seem happy to see me. Thinking myself maturely unselfish, I speculated that perhaps he had weeds or bugs in his garden.

"So, are we done talking about the research?" Chris said.

"Yes," I replied and rose to leave.

"Then I have something else to say," he said, adjusting his chair to face me squarely. "Listen, Jessica. That really hurt. Please don't do that again."

My blank stare told him I didn't get it.

"I was expecting you to work in the lab this summer," he said.

"I know, Chris, but I just couldn't do it," I said.

"Yes, I understand that. I'm just telling you that it was hurtful to me, and please don't do it again."

I tried to reply, but there was nothing to say.

"Do you know why I love the birdsong lab so

much?" he said.

"Because we're discovering things about bird-song," I foolishly replied.

"No, Jessica. I love it because, more than anything else, I love education and seeing students grow and being part of that."

I sat in silence for a while, trying to muster the courage to speak. "I'm sorry, Chris," I said, meaning an apology for perhaps the first time in my life.

"Okay," he said. "It's okay."

And that was it. We walked together back to the lab.

"So, do you know why capuchin monkeys clean each other?" he asked me.

Before my eyes, Chris had been transformed from a teacher to a person. And I had just gotten one of the biggest lessons of my life: My actions affected others, and what's more, they affected people I cared about.

Senior year came and went, and at the end, I had a thesis on mockingbird song. Chris sat in support while I nervously presented my work to a board of professors, somehow managing to whistle birdsong through my shaky voice. I told them about the patterns we had identified and how the birds used a repetition of song cycles to communicate. They awarded me high honors.

Chris's graduation present to me was a book

about birds that he had published under a pen name. Full of rich observations told in a friendly narrative, the book was part of Chris's life outside of academics, which is why he had used a pen name. As a gift, it was Chris's way of telling me that I had become a part of his life.

Chris had taught me many things in the three years I spent at the birdsong lab. He taught me to think critically and to wonder at life and our ability to understand it. He taught me to look at causes, not just at end results. Through birdsong, he had connected me to the big world I was soon to meet. But perhaps his greatest gift to me was the simple, beautiful lesson that each person is a whole life and the glimpse we see of one another is never the entire picture.

There never was a paper published on our research. I later came to understand that it was unlikely any scientific journal would publish our work, because it was based on only one bird's song. Chris had known this all along.

—*Jessica Wapner*

Back to My Future

Long ago, on a planet far, far away, I used to make music for a living. Singing, songwriting, performing. But that was elsewhere, before marriage, before children. Before I learned that in order to be a real grown-up, one had to accommodate and generate a certain amount of seriousness in order to fit in properly with the adult world.

One day, on the planet where I now live, divorced and with my kids and employed as a Very Important Business Consultant, I was prospecting on the Internet for business clients. I happened to glance at an innocent classified ad: "Part time music specialist wanted for preschool." I could see it now. Millionaire's Row here I come. Not.

My bailiwick was boardrooms; leather chairs lined up against conference tables; offices equipped with networks, DSL, faxes, pagers, and cell phones; and discussions that rarely justified their length and bombast. I rushed home to be with the kids just in time for the nanny to leave. I missed their school events. We ordered out a lot. But the mortgage was paid.

During the endless dissolution of my marriage and subsequent tsunami of change, in the wake of which I became a single parent, the part of my heart where music came from seemed to float away. It was ballast thrown overboard. I had to bail water, check the keel, repair the sails. I could not let the children know how many leaks there were in our new life. There was no time, no room for music, for useless things.

Reading this ad seven years after my financially apocalyptic divorce, I was reminded of the pile of bills on my desk, overflowing like Strega Nona's magic pasta pot. All of my business training revolved around managing statistics and solvency, predicting income against costs, measuring labor and production. It was a cinch that even considering a low-paying teaching job was idiotic. There was only one thing to do.

I submitted my resume.

The preschool director called me. Before I could give myself time to come to my senses, I made an appointment for an interview the next day.

After some cursory face time, the director suggested, "Why don't we set up a class for you, so you can sing with the kids? That way, I can see how you teach."

"Right now?" I asked.

"Sure," she answered with the determined style of an administrator used to grabbing live bodies. I guess music teachers weren't exactly knocking down the finger-painted doors to get in.

On our way to the music room that, the director explained, doubled and tripled as a library and conference room, we passed a blur of pint-sized toddlers clattering down the linoleum hallway. Next to collages on the walls made of mud and sticks from the yard were butcher paper murals splashed with amoeba-shaped splotches of color, labeled, "This is the *tyrannosaurus rex* who eats my macaroni," and "Me in space with the backward pizza."

A few minutes after we arrived at our destination, ten tiny tornadoes tumbled into the room. I had nary a whiteboard nor a power suit to impress the clients. The children sat on the industrial-strength carpeting, each on a lily pad rug remnant, and looked up at me expectantly. Ten futures were at my command. For ten uncharted hearts, the next few moments were whatever I chose them to be. In my jeans, ponytail, comfortable baggy blouse, and flats, I sat down on the carpet and faced the panel of judges. The room smelled like plastic lamination and cookies being baked in the adjoining kitchen. I lifted both hands toward the ceiling and started to sing, "Two hands up!" They followed along like perfect fuzzy ducklings.

I knew then and there that among their curious eyes, baby hair, scraped knees, Batman T-shirts, and untouched hope was my own future.

The director apologized as she revealed the part-time hourly wage. It was about a fourth of what I was making. I mustered all my business negotiating skills and asked, "When do I start?"

After I had been teaching for several months, I retrieved a mysterious orange parchment envelope from my state-of-the-art music teacher's Pendaflex folder, which hung in a cardboard box. Inside was a printed card that read,

> *One hundred years from now it will not matter*
> *What kind of car I drove,*
> *What kind of house I lived in,*
> *How much money I had in my bank account,*
> *Nor what my clothes looked like.*
> *But the world may be a little better,*
> *Because I was important in the life of a child.*

Tucked next to the card was an American Express check for one hundred dollars. It was from the parents' association. In spite of the simple corniness of the words, my neophyte teacher's heart fluttered with gratitude at such a considerate acknowledgment. I tacked the card to my home office wall, joining the recent collection of photos of singing children and thank-you notes from teachers, children, and parents. In celebration of the unexpected and much-needed hundred dollars, I bought two monstrous portobello mushrooms as a special side dish for our dinner and put the rest of the money in my savings account.

I have had to practice the sound of "teacher." It is not grand, like "vice president of business management." It sounds unimpressive at parties. But most of the parties I now attend involve the hot dog song, egg-shaped rhythm instruments, and red plastic chopsticks banging on drums made from paper plates. And I never thank anyone that it's Friday, because at the end of each week I am sorry to wave good-bye to the tiny clients who have given me back my future. And whose futures I may have touched as well.

—*Jolie Kanat*

"Back to My Future" was first published in the March 2003 issue of *Skirt Magazine*.

The Broken Heart

As a child I remember being very smart. Figuring out things and learning how they worked came easy to me. But learning to read turned into a heartbreaking chore.

While all the other children sat in a big circle in that second grade Chicago classroom and read from their books, I squirmed in an isolated chair against the wall, an Alice and Jerry reader resting in my lap. Miss Johnson, my special education teacher, smiled sweetly as her finger went gliding from word to word, her red fingernail polish sharply contrasting the black squiggles tracking the page.

"See Jerry run," she said, her musical voice falling ever so slightly.

"See Jerry run," I repeated mechanically as my eyes followed her lovely finger across the page from squiggle to squiggle.

To me, those squiggles represented little more than mysterious smudges. For all I knew, the words on that page could have been Egyptian hieroglyphics.

Because of Arkansas poverty and limited educational opportunities, I missed my first two years of school. Truancy laws were lax in the rural areas, and the nearest school was more than thirty miles away with no bus route. Few questions were asked in that part of the country. Everyone pretty much minded his own business.

But the family was growing; I was the oldest of five kids. So Dad, determined that his children would not grow up as ignorant and uneducated as he had, quit his job on the farm and moved us all to Chicago. There, he received training under the GI Bill and found a good job as a welder in one of the local factories. I started school in the second grade at the age of seven.

Each day, while the other students read in their circle and eyed me with suspicion and hatred, Miss Johnson would sit with me and guide me through my lessons. Week after week, page after page, we plodded through that thin reader.

Sometimes, I would recognize a word on my own, and Miss Johnson would become excited and reward me with a smile and a pat on the head. She made me feel very smart.

One day I recited an entire line without help,

and Miss Johnson hugged me. Her slender arms enwrapped me like soft honeysuckle vines; her closeness filled my nostrils with the smell of soap and perfume and ironed cotton. Her praise echoed in my ears like the chiming of a beautiful bell, tolling the inevitable death of my ignorance.

Miss Johnson was the most beautiful person in my world. Her soft blonde hair swished around her shoulders like golden straw in a windy wheat field. Her lovely smile and kind eyes sparkled like a halo on the head of an angel.

Yes, I loved her, and I wanted more: more reading, more praise, more hugs. I wanted a lot more hugs.

And I was smart, so I studied harder. Working with Mother after school, I expanded my knowledge of words. I discovered a rhythm and a cadence in basic structure, and I practiced sounding out syllables. All to impress my beautiful reading coach and perhaps earn another hug.

Then one day in late spring I accomplished my goal: Without her assistance and totally on my own, I read an entire page. Miss Johnson was so ecstatic, I thought she might explode with joy. Excited by my progress, she urged me to continue reading. My love for Miss Johnson carried me onward. Syllable after syllable. Word after word. Sentence after sentence. I read until I had completed several pages. Miss Johnson hugged me until my heart pounded. Finally, she stood up, holding my hand and smiling with those lovely lips.

"Don," she said. "I'm so proud of you. You are one of the smartest students I've ever coached. I want to thank you for working so hard and for allowing me to help you learn to read."

I must have smiled from ear to ear. Chair legs scraped the floor as the other students turned around to glare at me. I could feel their hatred growing, but I didn't care. My world glowed with brightness and happiness.

Then, Miss Johnson said, "Now that the hard part of your training is over, it's time for you to move to a higher level of reading. It's time for you to join the other students. And it's time for me to say good-bye."

My world went silent. I heard nothing as she quickly led me to the reading circle. I felt nothing as she patted me on the head. I saw nothing as the other students stopped glaring.

A little blonde girl brought another chair, and the students made a space for me in their group. As I sat down, they all started smiling at me. I became the center of attention. I was one of them now. In a blur of perfume and ironed cotton, Miss Johnson and her beautiful blonde hair disappeared out the classroom door. I never saw her lovely face again.

That day marked the real beginning of my education. I learned how to read, how to make new friends, and how not to cry when my heart was breaking. I also learned that if I'd been really smart, I wouldn't have been so smart.

Later that day the little blonde girl showed me how to cut a butterfly from a piece of folded construction paper. It took me three tries to get it right, but when I finished, the little blonde girl clapped her hands and gave me a hug.

—*Don Mitchell*

Last One Out

The traffic is light at 4:45 A.M. He zips to the golf course first. After putting in an hour and a half at that job, he is back on the expressway by 6:30. Down through the back streets of Philadelphia to pick up a student and on to the high school by 7:10. Up three flights of stairs, unlock the classroom door, and by 7:30, he has started another day at Edison High School. Not a bad morning for a fifty-seven-year-old man.

Inner-city Philadelphia is a tough place. The kids are tough because life hasn't dealt them the privileges that living in the suburbs offers. Their home life can be smattered with broken families and constant change. Hope is not always evident. Young girls too often become young mothers, and young boys don't always live long enough to become young men. Going to school could offer them a way out, but first they have to get through those four years. Their start is the freshman seminar class, with Bob Schlicht- mann as their teacher. Now, they have a chance.

"Mr. S," as he is known in the hallways, would not be happy in the well-to-do suburbs of Pennsylvania. That is for a different type of teacher. He chooses to teach in the inner city because children there are often the first ones in their families to have a chance at success. But it is not the Ivy League he shoots for. Graduation for them is being able to break out of the poverty and escape the influence of the street.

I met Bob Schlichtmann in the summer of 1965. We had grown up in neighboring towns. He had just completed his freshman year at college, and I had just graduated from high school. He was studying to be a teacher at the University of Toledo on a baseball scholarship. But in 1968 young men fresh out of col- lege who didn't have the means to go to graduate school were getting drafted. We parted, and Bob became a captain in the United States Marine Corps. He served for four years, which included a tour of duty in Vietnam. Then came marriage and six chil- dren. A teacher's salary doesn't go that far, so he fol- lowed a different profession for the next thirty years.

At fifty-one, he changed direction and went into teaching. But he wanted to teach only the ones who needed him most.

Freshman seminar class stands to be the most

pivotal course at Edison High School. There, students learn how to get along with each other, how to have a dialogue instead of a battle. Bob has nine months to teach them that words are the tools for expressing themselves and that writing gives them a way to personalize how and where they want to go. He teaches them that the world is about how to get along with different people, how to express themselves with words (not violence), and how to acquire a job that lets them stand on their own. He teaches them to take chances with their minds. It is not the grade they make, but the effort to make themselves better that he encourages.

The attention span of the kids can be short, so the energy level in the classroom must be high. The seminar class is tied in with Bob's world history class, and it is filled with hands-on projects. They make pyramids, sew Renaissance costumes, and act out the writing of the Declaration of Independence. Students coming to this class and you are not bored.

In his own boyhood high school, Bob was a top athlete, a jock. Baseball was his passion. Now, still fit and active, sports have given way to computers. His philosophy is that if each student can master and operate a computer, he or she can get a job. A job can take these students out of poverty. And then they stand a chance. His goal is to get each student trained on a computer so that he or she has the opportunity to take care of him or herself. And he has a plan.

Working with the National Cristina Foundation, a nonprofit organization that accepts donations of used computers, Bob spends his weekend afternoons and many a weekday evening driving through Pennsylvania, New Jersey, and Delaware, picking up donated computers. He brings them to school and his home and gets them into working shape. He has students with whom he has worked help him after school to get the computers in running order and connected to the Internet. Many of the computers are used in the classroom, but the rest are used for something even better.

Bob has put into effect a reward program. When a student has accomplished deserving work or makes an extra effort or just shows that he or she is trying, Bob gives that student a computer of his or her own. He offers students an opportunity to put themselves in touch with the world, and he enables them to learn that there are possibilities and imaginable options out there if they are willing to try. Being given a computer by their teacher raises their self-esteem and gives them hope that they can succeed, which is the best possible tool a teacher can give his students. They are being prepared to get a decent job.

When I heard Bob Schlichtmann was a teacher, I wasn't surprised. Bob was always the leader in high school, in college, and in the Marines. He invariably looked out for the ones less fortunate than him, and he never went for the big glory. You could count on Bob to do the job. He was always the last one out.

Oh, and there is still that other job at the golf course. He is back there at 7:00 P.M. weeknights and again on weekends to caddy. It may be difficult to live monetarily on a teacher's salary, but you can live with pride and gratification. Because you are a teacher.

—*Priscilla Whitley*

Tell Your Story in the Next *Cup of Comfort*!

We hope you have enjoyed *A Cup of Comfort for Teachers* and that you will share it with all the special people in your life.

You won't want to miss our next heartwarming volumes, *A Cup of Comfort for Sisters* and *A Cup of Comfort Devotional*. Look for these new books in your favorite bookstores soon!

We're brewing up lots of other *Cup of Comfort* books, each filled to the brim with true stories that will touch your heart and soothe your soul. The inspiring tales included in these collections are written by everyday men and women, and we would love to include one of your stories in an upcoming edition of *A Cup of Comfort*.

Do you have a powerful story about an experience that dramatically changed or enhanced your life? A compelling story that can stir our emotions, make us think, and bring us hope? An inspiring story that reveals lessons of humility within a vividly told tale? Tell us your story!

Each *Cup of Comfort* contributor will receive a monetary fee, author credit, and a complimentary copy of the book. Just e-mail your submission of 1,000 to 2,000 words (one story per e-mail; no attachments, please) to:

cupofcomfort@adamsmedia.com

Or, if e-mail is unavailable to you, send it to:

A Cup of Comfort
Adams Media
57 Littlefield Street
Avon, MA 02322

You can submit as many stories as you'd like, for whichever volumes you'd like. Make sure to include your name, address, and other contact information and indicate for which volume you'd like your story to be considered. We also welcome your suggestions or stories for new *Cup of Comfort* themes.

For more information, please visit our Web site: *www.cupofcomfort.com.*

We look forward to sharing many more soothing *Cups of Comfort* with you!

Contributors

Michelle (Mann) Adserias ("In the Light of a Master") was born and raised in Wisconsin Rapids, Wisconsin. She received her secondary teaching certificate in communications at the University of Wisconsin, Stevens Point. She now resides with her husband, Peter, in Menasha, Wisconsin. They have four children: Ryan, Kyle, Madeline, and Hannah.

Greg Beatty ("Because It Matters") has held an assortment of odd jobs, including massage therapist and bartender on a charter boat. He supports his writing habit by teaching for the University of Phoenix Online. When he's not at his computer, he enjoys cooking, practicing martial arts, and having complex interpersonal relationships.

Kathy Briccetti, Ph.D. ("The Power of One"), works as a school psychologist in Oakland, California, and as a freelance writer from her Berkeley home. Her writing has appeared in newspapers and magazines and on public radio. She is at work on a memoir about her search for roots among three generations of absent fathers and adoption in her family.

Harriet Cooper ("I Speak, You Speak, We All Speak English . . . Eventually") is an instructor of English as a second language (ESL) for the Toronto (Canada) District School Board. She has written humorous and technical articles on teaching that have appeared in national newspapers and educational newsletters, and she has written and edited several educational handbooks.

Vicki Cox ("Guns and Roses") retired from public teaching in 2000. Since then, she has written four children's biographies for Chelsea House Publishing and one anthology, *Rising Stars and Ozark Constellations*, a collection of essays about the nation's heartland. She hangs her clothes in Lebanon, Missouri, but mostly lives in her car.

Jacqueline D. Cross ("The Joy of Learning") lives in Connecticut with her husband, children, dog, and cat, where she works as an office manager for elderly residential housing. When not being Mom, she can be found cloistered in her den, writing—that is, when she is able to kick one of her kids off the computer.

Diana Davis ("Extra Credit") is the assistant director of admissions at the University of Missouri-St. Louis. She holds undergraduate and master's degrees in writing, and her poetry, short stories, and articles have appeared in numerous periodicals. A mother of three grown daughters and grandmother of two, she lives quietly with her dog in Florissant, Missouri.

Rita DiCarne ("From Intro to Coda") teaches music and language arts at St. Catherine's school in Horsham, Pennsylvania. A fellow of the Pennsylvania Writing project, DiCarne resides in Horsham with her husband, Chuck, and children, Angela and Charlie. Her articles have appeared in *Today's Catholic Teacher*.

Cecilia M. Dobbs ("The Beauty Beneath") currently teaches sixth-grade science in the South Bronx. She plans to start journalism school and hopes to write for the science section of a New York newspaper. She lives in Manhattan.

Samantha Ducloux ("Grieving the F"), a lifelong teacher and student of many things, including languages, family relationships, writing, and dance, has published fiction and nonfiction under the names Samellyn Wood and Samantha Ducloux. She lives with her husband in Portland, Oregon, where she is learning to grieve the Fs and celebrate the As.

Julie Dunbar ("Grade School Lessons for a Lifetime") is a Colorado-based freelance writer. She tracked down her fourth-grade teacher after having children of her own. She found that Mr. Sparato's laugh lines were a little deeper and that he was even more generous, genuine, and silly than she had remembered.

Kathleen Edwards ("Show-and-Tell") left behind the teaching life many years ago and is now a wife and artist. She lives in the Blue Ridge Mountains of Virginia, where she indulges in ceramics, painting, and writing.

James Eisenstock ("A Lesson Learned") is an Air Corps veteran who flew twenty-six missions in World War II. He shares a home in South Hadley, Massachusetts, and two sons, two daughters-in-law, and two grandchildren with his wife of nearly sixty years. He enjoys golf and creative writing.

Madeleine Enns ("Walk Softly, Children Working"), a retired teacher, lives in Winnipeg, Canada. Her stories have been published in several magazines, including *Rhubarb* and *Sophia*.

Kathleen Ewing ("A Pair of Nothings") was an aerospace manufacturing engineer when the world tilted on its axis on September 11, 2001. Now an office coordinator, she resides in Arizona's central mountains, where she enjoys horseback riding, target shooting, and four-wheeling the back country in her Dodge pickup truck.

A. Ferreri ("Dial A for Effort") teaches English as a second language (ESL) at a school in Wisconsin to kids aged eleven to fifteen from Mexico, Puerto Rico, Asia, and Africa, who struggle daily to conquer both a new language and a new culture.

Dawn FitzGerald ("There's No Substitute") is a freelance writer and substitute teacher in Cleveland, Ohio. She is the author of five biographies for children: *Angela Bassett, Ben Stiller,* and *Destiny's Child* for Chelsea House Publishers; and *Julia Butterfly Hill: Saving the Redwoods* and *Robert Ballard: Discovering the Titanic and Beyond* for the Millbrook Press.

Tammy Glaser ("A Spoonful of Sugar"), a 1985 graduate of the United States Naval Academy, lives in Minnesota with her husband, Steve, and children, Pamela and David. She runs an e-mail list for families homeschooling autistic children.

Whitney L. Grady ("Why I Teach") resides in Kinston, North Carolina, with her husband, James, and their dog, Shug, where she teaches seventh and eighth grade at Arendell Parrott Academy. She gains inspiration for her writing from her students, friends, family, and weekends at the beach. This is her first published story.

Michele Griskey ("Pass It On") lives with her family on Orcas Island, Washington, where she writes and teaches writing for the University of Phoenix. In her free time, she gardens and makes up stories with her two young sons.

Elisabeth Rose Gruner ("Mama Mentor") teaches English and women's studies at the University of Richmond, Richmond, Virginia. Her academic writing has been published in *SIGNS: Journal of Women in Culture and Society, Children's Literature,* and other periodicals. Her personal writing has been featured in magazines and anthologies, including *Brain, Child: The Magazine for Thinking Mothers* and *Toddler: Real-Life Stories of Those Fickle, Urgent, Irrational, Tiny People We Love* (Seal Press).

Evan Guilford-Blake ("Field Trip") is an award-winning, nationally produced playwright and professional storyteller who has also published short fiction, poetry, and journalism. He lives in the Atlanta, Georgia, area with his wife (and inspiration) Roxanna, a jewelry designer and freelance writer, and their two doves, Quill and Gabriella.

Glenn Hameroff ("Testing My Mettle") is a retired teacher living in Delray Beach, Florida. With the advance of Parkinson's disease, writing became the focus of his retirement. He believes that humor is a necessary tool to enrich the classroom.

Mikki Hollinger ("Champion of Children"), a native of New Orleans, resides in Atlanta, Georgia, with her husband. A healthcare project manager by trade, she considers herself, without hesitation, a writer. This is her first published work and a tribute to her favorite teacher, her mother.

Julie A. Kaiser ("Flight Dreams") is a freelance writer who still stargazes each night. She lives in Chatham, Illinois, with her husband, Scott, and son, Jakob. She received her MFA in creative writing from Southern Illinois University.

Carol L. F. Kampf ("What This Teacher Understands") holds two master's degrees, one in counseling, and is the owner of a human resources consulting firm. She lives with her husband and two sons in Alpharetta, Georgia. Her writing has appeared in several publications, including *Attention Magazine*, the *Harrisburg Patriot News*, and ParentToParent.com.

Jolie Kanat ("Back to My Future") is a music specialist, mom, producer of two original children's music CDs, and author. She now teaches everything from the hot dog song to Beethoven to hundreds of young children in the San Francisco Bay Area, in California.

Erin K. Kilby ("Lost and Found") is a freelance writer who resides in Kingwood, Texas. She teaches English and enjoys writing, reading, crocheting, and spending time with her husband, Michael, her stepson, Tyler, and her dog, Chelsea. Her stories have appeared in anthologies and magazines, including *Reminisce*, *Obadiah*, and *Your Family*.

Debbi Klopman ("What I Never Learned in Kindergarten") is an immigration lawyer in Great Neck, New York, where she lives with her husband, Tom, and her eighteen-year-old son, Jeremy. While the rest of the world is sleeping, she writes stories.

Christine Guidry Law ("Lizard Boy") is an elementary school teacher, freelance writer, and editor of *Baton Rouge Parents* magazine. She lives with her husband and three children in Zachary, Louisiana. She now homeschools six children in kindergarten, first, and fifth grades.

Emmarie Lehnick ("Ant Bites"), of Amarillo, Texas, is a retired English/speech teacher who holds both a bachelor's and a master's degree. She and her husband have a daughter, a son, and four grandsons. She is a member of Inspiration Writers Alive.

Beverly Carol Lucey ("Snapshots"), originally from New England, now writes from the Land of Lard and Peaches, having chosen to follow her husband south, to Arkansas. Like Flannery O'Connor, she knew that the line from the old song was true: "A good man is hard to find."

George Malsam ("I Can't Read") taught senior high industrial arts for twenty-seven years in Denver, Colorado. He holds a master's degree in education, a bachelor of arts degree in industrial arts education, and an associate's degree in building construction technology from Oklahoma State University. Now retired, he teaches woodworking skills to his nine grandchildren in his home woodshop.

Don Mitchell ("The Broken Heart"), originally from rural Arkansas, now lives in West Monroe, Louisiana, with his charming wife, Dixie. As freelance telecommunication engineers, Don and Dixie travel around the country solving industry problems. In their spare time they enjoy singing karaoke, performing stand-up comedy, and writing funny movie reviews.

Mary Paliescheskey ("A Matter of Trust") lives in Southern California with her family. Once upon a time, she was a research scientist. Today, she is homeschooling her three sons—hoping to follow in Mr. Roach's footsteps.

Tony Phillips ("They Wanted to Teach") is a middle school science teacher from Indiana. In 2003, he published his first novel, *Superior Species: Evolution Defies Creation*, a

Christian science-fiction novel addressing the real-life conflict between science and religion, through PublishAmerica. He also writes short stories.

Hattie Mae Ratliff ("The Gift"), a mother of three and grandmother of four, has been writing for many years but only six years ago began sharing her stories, often about children, with the world. She makes her home in San Marcos, Texas.

Cheryl Reed, Ph.D. ("Piranha Class"), has taught at the high school, community college, and university levels. She has published articles and presented seminars on teaching strategies and has written or coedited several books. Her deep love is teaching students to think things through and to communicate their ideas to people who need to hear them.

Tanya M. Showen ("Moment of Truth") resides in East Texas with her husband, Keith. She wrote this story in honor of her second-grade teacher, Loretta Vancleave.

K. Anne Smith ("Clown School") is a retired speech/language pathologist who currently teaches public speaking at the college level. Her short stories, poems, and articles have appeared in numerous magazines, including *BlueRidge Country*, *GreenPrints*, and *Family Fun*.

Thomas Smith ("Innocence and the Divine") has a wife he is crazy about and two dogs that are (mostly) housebroken. He is an award-winning writer, reporter, TV news producer, playwright, and pretty fair banjo picker. He divides his time between Raleigh and Topsail Island, North Carolina.

Paula Sword ("The Sound of One Door Opening"), a speech pathologist for twenty-two years, lives in McDonough, Georgia, with her husband, Lyle; three children, Noah, Matt, and Danielle; and bassett hound, Copper. She enjoys expressing herself through writing and photography and gets inspiration from her students and their parents, friends, and family.

Annemarieke Tazelaar ("A Little Child Shall Lead Them"), after years of teaching, now owns her own business and spends her spare time writing. Several of her stories have been published in A Cup of Comfort books.

Susan B. Townsend ("The First Day") is a writer and stay-at-home mother. Transplanted from the west coast of Canada six years ago, she now makes her home on a 300-acre farm in southeastern Virginia with her husband, five children, and a zoo full of animals. Her nonfiction work has appeared in several anthologies, including other volumes of A Cup of Comfort, and her fiction can be found in numerous e-zines.

Bonnie L. Walker ("Last Day" and "The Educated Dude") is the author of several language arts textbooks. Her articles have appeared in the *Washington Post* and other publications. She enjoys yoga, tennis, and playing games with her grandchildren. Her most significant years were spent as a middle school teacher.

Jessica Wapner ("Truth and Consequence") works as the managing editor of a New York-based medical publisher. She is also the publisher of *Fizz*, a quarterly newsletter dedicated to putting right, generative works of writing out into the world. She lives in Brooklyn, New York, with her sweetheart and a feisty cat.

Abby Warmuth ("The Creative One") grew up in Dearborn, Michigan, and now resides in Fort Mill, South Carolina. After earning a bachelor's degree in English from the University of Michigan, Ann Arbor, she worked for nine years with a *Fortune* 500 company. An aspiring writer, she now teaches "left behind" students at Central Piedmont Community College.

Katherine L. E. White ("The Other Two Chairs") is an anthropologist living in Charlotte, North Carolina. When she isn't writing fiction, essays, or poetry, she is immersed in the world of small children as a kindergarten teacher.

Priscilla Whitley ("Last One Out") studied journalism at the University of Missouri and enjoys writing autobiographical essays and stories about the extraordinary experiences of "real" people. A freelance writer, she also manages a gourmet cooking store and cooking school in Ridgefield, Connecticut, where she lives with a dog, a cat, and a horse. Her daughter attends college in Massachusetts.

Melissa Scholes Young ("What Teaching Justin Taught Me") is an educator whose teaching experiences range from an international school in Brazil to working with vocational students in Appalachia. She is currently an adjunct professor of English at Eastern Connecticut State University. When not teaching or writing, she loves to read, practice yoga, and spend time with her husband and daughter.

About the Editor

Colleen Sell has long believed in the power of story to connect us with our inner spirits, the Higher Spirit, and one another. Her passion for storytelling has been inspired and nurtured by many teachers and mentors, a gift she is paying forward by helping others to share their stories.

The editor of more than sixty published books, Colleen has also authored and ghostwritten several books. She has been a magazine editor, journalist, columnist, essayist, and copywriter.

She lives with her husband, T. N. Trudeau, in a nineteenth-century Victorian home on a forty-acre lavender and tree farm in the Pacific Northwest, where she writes tales both tall and true.

Also Available in the . . .

Each *Cup of Comfort* book features over 50 exceptional stories of ordinary people who have overcome great obstacles, persevered through thick and through thin, and found the power to control their own destinies. Readers will laugh and cry out loud as they share in the many moving experiences detailed within these pages.

ISBN: 1-58062-524-X
Trade Paperback, $9.95

ISBN: 1-58062-622-X
Trade Paperback, $9.95

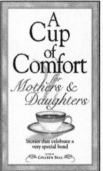

ISBN: 1-58062-844-3
Trade Paperback, $9.95